AUSTRALIAN FLY PATTERNS

BY PETER COULSON

AFN
AUSTRALIAN FISHING NETWORK

First published in 2004 by
Australian Fishing Network Pty Ltd
48 Centre Way, South Croydon VIC 3136
Telephone: 03 9761 4044 Facsimile: 03 9761 4055
Email: sales@afn.com.au
Website: www.afn.com.au

Designed by: Neetu Patel

ISBN 186513063-X

Foreword

I was recently fishing near Potters Point on the shore of Victoria's Lake Bullen Merri. It was late on a grey autumn afternoon. Muz Wilson, whose name appears beside some significant patterns in this book, had dispatched an urgent order of flies and was now free to join me. Muz's station wagon pulled up just as I tied on a pattern very similar to his Merri Minnow. The fly change was the latest strategy in what was becoming a forlorn quest to catch a particular smelter, which had been moving sporadically all afternoon. For the umpteenth time, I cast as far as I could out over the steely water, let the new fly sink for ten seconds, then began a slow figure-of-eight retrieve.

There are no snags beyond the bottomless drop-off at Bullen Merri, but even so, when I felt dead resistance soon after the retrieve began, for a moment I thought 'log' or 'weed'. Then the supposed snag began to move away from me with steady, irresistible power. It was several stressful minutes later that the fish finally broke the surface. The sickle tail and brilliant silver flank immediately revealed it as a chinook salmon, and by far the largest I had ever hooked. The salmon still pulled stubbornly against the bend of the rod, but it stayed near the surface, and at some point I began to count it as caught. Murray reached for the camera while I unsnipped the landing net from the catch on my vest. And then the hook pulled. Just like that. No mighty leaps or sudden lunges. One moment, I had a fish of a lifetime on the end, the next moment I did not.

Some time has now passed since that day at Bullen Merri. The therapy sessions are coming along nicely, and the nightmares—where I discover too late that all my fly hooks have turned from metal to wood—are becoming less frequent. In fact I'm even capable of analytically reviewing the loss of the giant salmon, and planning a return visit.

One of the questions that flits through my mind (though now less obsessively) is, how important was the fly itself? A further hour spent fishing with it failed to get another response, and it was actually a Woolly Bugger that caught me a consolation brown on dark.

Ahh, flies and fish. Do some patterns just happen to be in the right place at the right time, or do they truly exude an indefinable magic that makes them great? At least some flies most probably fall into the latter category. Look at the variations on the Tom Jones theme in this book. Either John Lanchester was really on to something when he designed the Tommy, or the fly fishing world is full of deluded people (myself included!)

Some of the flies in this book were devised by experts as famous as the names of the flies themselves, others by anglers who are probably not nearly as well known as they deserve to be. As I flick through the pages, looking at Peter Coulson's virtually three-dimensional photographs, some patterns are as familiar as the faces of old friends, while others are strangers who I would dearly love to meet. I can't really explain how I can look at a fly I've never seen before and know it will catch fish, but within these pages, that has happened many times.

To my mind, this book defies simple classification. It is not a book of all flies, nor the best flies (whatever the heck they are), or even the most popular flies. But it is definitely a book full of important and worthwhile flies. No fly angler can really ask for more than that.

Philip Weigall

Preface

After decades on the banks of lakes, rivers, estuaries and oceans, I count myself as very lucky—I have made a large number of friendships while fishing that have endured over the years. Most fly anglers are approachable, friendly and willing to share their knowledge with another interested angler.

As a professional fly tier and angler my interest was always aroused as to what flies the anglers were actually using, especially in waters with which they were familiar and successful. As most fly anglers consider themselves part of a very large family they were usually pleased to show the fly that they had tied and with which they had caught fish.

In many cases the tier wasn't a professional fly tier and made-do with the materials that were on hand at the time. If these flies caught fish then they were fished with even more confidence, and that particular pattern variant became a favourite and was repeatedly tied and used. At other times, the fly was a favourite, and sometimes secret pattern.

Over these decades of encounters with fellow anglers the seeds of this book were sown and grew. This book is not a definitive reference book or a dictionary of Australian fly patterns. It's a collection of fly patterns gathered from Australian fly tiers and, more importantly, fly fisherman. Many of the patterns in this book are slight variations to a more-famous original. This was the tie that the angler was catching fish on at the time and that is what I have tried to capture and show here.

Many of the original flies that I received where in poor condition as they had been collected from fisherman in the field and the flies were not showpieces, but were tools of the angler's trade. They had been fished with and came straight off the line or from the fly patch on the vest. Where the fly was no longer in suitable condition to photograph, with help from Adam Royter, Ezra Bibby and Michael Milczuk we tried to recreate the tie as closely as possible to the pattern we had been given. Any deviations in the pattern from the original are not intentional and I apologise for any misrepresentation.

Acknowledgements

This book is a collection of the ideas, work and sweat of many anglers. These special thanks are to those who provided me with additional help, inspiration and pushed me to complete this book. Adam Royter, Ezra Bibby, Michael Milczuk, David Dodd, Philip Weigall, Rick Keam, Mick Hall. The Australian Fishing Network owners and employees. And all the fly anglers who donated their time, flies and knowledge to this book.

Peter Coulson took all of the photographs of the flies in this book.

Other photographs are the work of: Bill Classon, Adam Royter, Greg Cooper, Stephen Booth, Dave Hodge, Chris Parkinson, Peter Coulson.

Contents

SECTION ONE

TROUT

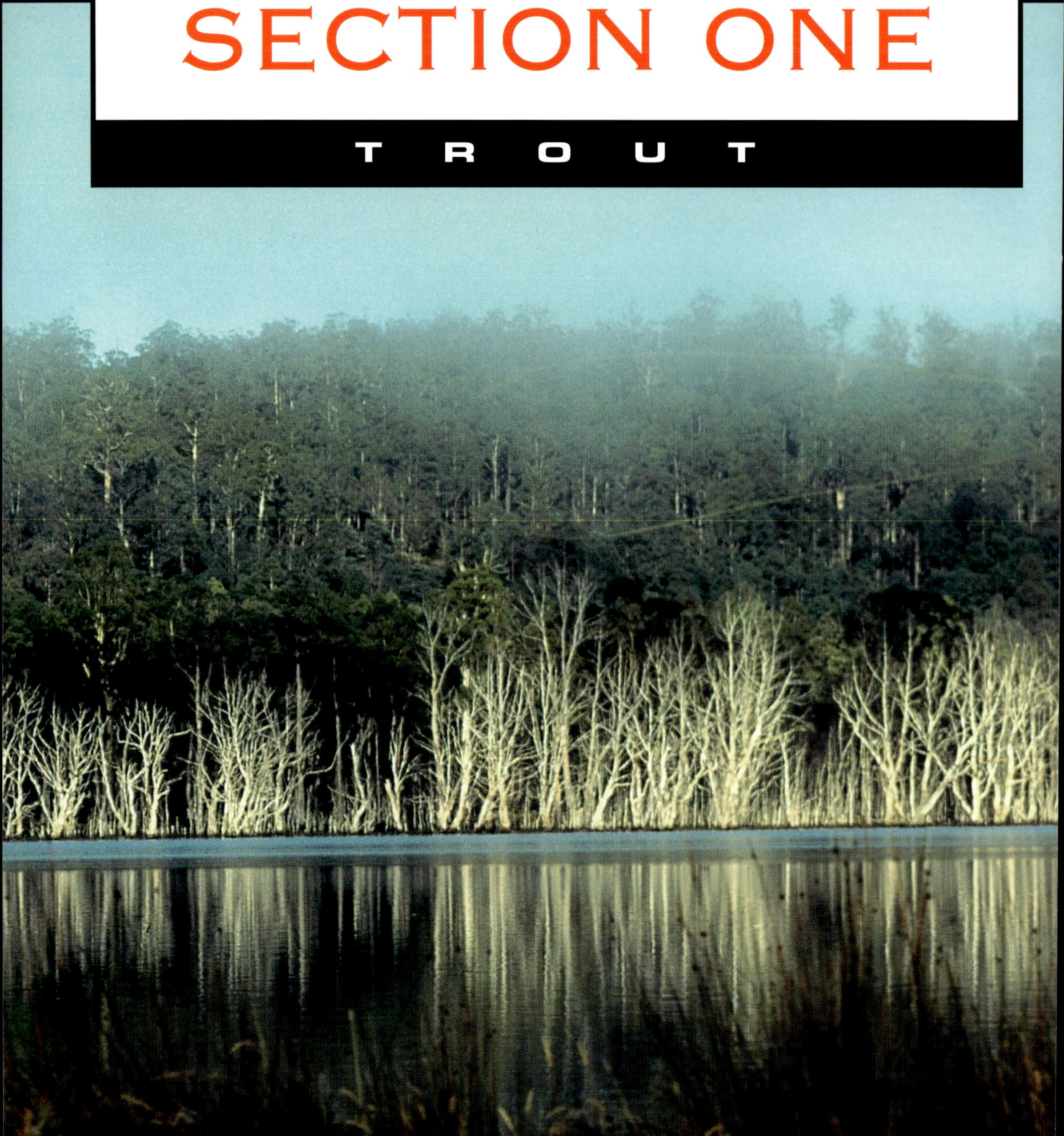

CHAPTER 1

BEETLES

ADAM'S GUM BEETLE

HOOK: Dry fly, size 8–14
THREAD: Yellow 6/0
BODY: Olive green Antron dubbing
OVERBODY: Yellow closed cell foam with red marker at the butt
LEGS: Yellow Flexi Floss

This fly will float all day, so it is excellent for fast or broken water.

Tied by Adam Royter

BLACK BEETLE

HOOK: Kamasan B401, size 12–14
THREAD: Black
TAG: White, red or yellow Uni-Yarn
BODY: Peacock herl
HACKLE: Brown or black hen
FEELERS: Pheasant tail
BACK: Black Evasote (dry fly foam)

Tied by David Dodd

BLACK BEETLE WET

HOOK: Kamasan B160, size 12–16
THREAD: Black
UNDERBODY: Copper wire
BODY: Black wool
WINGCASE: Black crow feather fibres
BEARD: Black hackle fibres

Tied by Gerd Behnecke

BROWN BEETLE WET

HOOK: Kamasan B160, size 12–16
THREAD: Black
UNDERBODY: Copper wire
BODY: Fiery brown seal's fur
WINGCASE: Black crow feather fibres

Tied by Gerd Behnecke

Tied by Peter Coulson

BLACK FOAM BEETLE

HOOK: Kamasan B401, size 12–14
THREAD: Black
BODY: Fine black dubbing
BACK: Black closed cell foam
LEGS: Black Flexi Floss

Tied by Noel Jetson

DEERHAIR BEETLE, BLACK

HOOK: Dry fly, size 10–14
THREAD: Black
BODY: Black deer hair, spun and clipped
HACKLE: Black cock hackle

Tied by Noel Jetson

DEERHAIR BEETLE, BROWN

HOOK: Dry fly, size 10–14
THREAD: Black
BODY: Fiery brown deer hair, spun and clipped
HACKLE: Fiery brown cock hackle

Tied by Noel Jetson

DEERHAIR GUM BEETLE

HOOK: Dry fly, size 10–16
THREAD: Black
BODY: Yellow deer hair, spun and clipped
SHELLBACK: Green raffia
HACKLE: Furnace cock hackle

FAB BEETLE (Foam Arse Beetle)

HOOK: Dry fly, size 8–14
THREAD: Black 6/0
TAIL & UNDERBODY: Closed cell foam in black, red, yellow or white.
OVERBODY: Peacock herl
UNDER THE HACKLE: Dark brown dry fly dubbing
HACKLE: Brown and black cock clipped flat across the bottom

Put this fly down with a 'crunch' to alert fish. It won't sink because of the foam. It works well when the fly is on the water for a long time, or when few back casts are made.

Tied by Adam Royter

FOAM HEAD BEETLE

HOOK: Kamasan B401, size 10–14
THREAD: Black
UNDERBODY & HEAD: Black or grey closed cell foam
BODY: Peacock herl

Due to the foam body and head this fly will float all day. It is good for fast or broken water.

Tied by Adam Royter

GEEHI BEETLE

HOOK: Tiemco 102Y, size 13–17
THREAD: Black
TAIL: Golden pheasant tippets
BODY: Peacock herl palmered with red cock hackle
RIB: Fine gold wire
HEAD HACKLE: Red cock
HEAD: Black thread

The Geehi Beetle is particularly effective during late spring and summer when good numbers of beetles hatch around the rivers of northeast Victoria. It is also a good, general-purpose fly.

Tied by David Dodd

GREAT LAKE BEETLE

HOOK: Kamasan B401, size 10–14
THREAD: Black
BODY: Black cock hackle, palmered and trimmed
WING: Scarlet hackle tips
HACKLE: Scarlet cock

Tied by Michael Milczuk

Tied by David Dodd

GUM BEETLE (Variation)

HOOK: Tiemco 102Y, size 13–15
THREAD: Yellow
TAG: White
BODY: Yellow dry fly foam
THROAT HACKLE: Light tan hen
TYING: To complete this fly, colour with permanent marker to suit

Cast this fly to rising fish during beetle-fall along forested shores.

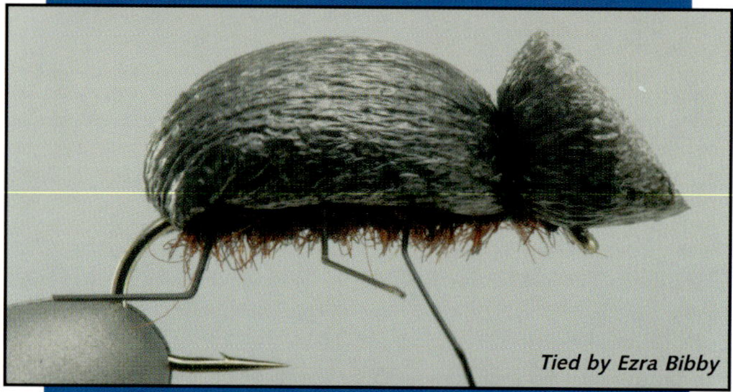

Tied by Ezra Bibby

HORSE HAIR BEETLE

HOOK: Kamasan B401, size 10–14
THREAD: Black
BODY: Fiery brown angora dubbing
LEGS: Horse tail hair kinked with a hot dubbing needle
SHELLBACK: Black closed cell foam
HEAD: Butt from shellback

This is a general beetle pattern, good around flooded lake margins. A white dot painted on the back of the fly makes it easier to keep track of this fly.

Tied by Peter Coulson

KIEWA CHRISTMAS BEETLE

HOOK: Dry fly, size 8–14
THREAD: Black 6/0
UNDERBODY: Black thread
OVERBODY: Black closed cell foam
HACKLE: Black cock clipped on top so that it swims upside down

This fly was designed by a couple of keen fly anglers on the Keiwa River one Christmas and had a great deal of success. It is best fished early morning when fish are mopping up the dead Christmas beetles that drowned overnight.

Tied by Noel Jetson

KELLY TAG

HOOK: Dry fly, size 10–14
THREAD: Black
TAG: Red Antron
BODY: Black deer hair, spun and clipped
HACKLE: Fiery brown cock hackle

MOVIE STAR

HOOK: Dry fly, size 10–16
THREAD: Black
BODY: Peacock herl
WINGPOST: HIVIS
HACKLE: Ginger or brown, dressed heavily

Tied by Ray Butterworth

ORANGE UPSIDEDOWN TAG

HOOK: Tiemco 102Y, size 13–15
THREAD: Black
TAIL: Orange wool
BODY: Peacock herl
HACKLE: Bright dyed orange grizzle, clipped on top

I don't know why, but this beetle pattern catches lots of fish.

Tied by Peter Coulson

RED TAG

HOOK: Tiemco 102Y, size 13–15
THREAD: Black
TAIL: Red wool
BODY: Peacock herl
HACKLE: Red cock

Tied by David Dodd

RED TAG DEER HAIR

HOOK: Tiemco 102Y, size 13–15
THREAD: Black
TAIL: Red wool
BODY: Black deer hair, spun and clipped
HEAD TAG: Red wool

Tied by Peter Coulson

RED TAG DEER HAIR

HOOK: Tiemco 102Y, size 13–15
THREAD: Black
TAIL: Red wool
BODY: Brown deer hair, spun and clipped
HEAD HACKLE: Red cock
HEAD: Black thread

Like most deer hair flies, this pattern floats very well in broken water.

RED TAG HIGH FLOATER

HOOK: Dry fly, size 10–14
THREAD: Black 6/0
TAG: Red Micro Crystal
UNDERBODY: Black closed cell foam
OVERBODY: Peacock herl
HACKLE: Brown and red cock

This fly will float all day, so it is excellent for fast or broken water. The flash in the tag works as an attractor on bright days.

RED TAG HIGH FLOATER

HOOK: Dry fly, size 8–14
THREAD: Black 6/0
TAG: Red floss
UNDERBODY: Black closed cell foam
OVERBODY: Peacock herl
HACKLE: Brown and black cock

This fly will float all day, so it is excellent for fast or broken water.

RED TAG PALMERED

HOOK: Tiemco 102Y, size 13–15
THREAD: Black
TAIL: Red wool
BODY: Peacock herl
RIB: Fine copper wire
BODY HACKLE: Red cock, smaller than head hackle
HEAD HACKLE: Red or brown cock
HEAD: Black thread

Cast this fly to rising fish, or drift across and down. The Red Tag Palmered rides higher in the runs and broken water.

RED TAG SEAL'S FUR

HOOK: Kamasan B401, size 10–14
THREAD: Black
TAG: Uni Stretch floss, Chinese red
BODY: Olive seal's fur
RIB: Fine gold wire
HACKLE: Fiery brown cock

Fish this to places where you think fish may be holding—alongside logs, through bubble-lines and around rocks. You can also sit it in front of cruising fish.

Tied by Ezra Bibby

SCARAB BEETLE

HOOK: Dry fly, size 8–14
THREAD: Dark brown 6/0
UNDERBODY: Dark brown thread
OVERBODY & HEAD: Closed cell foam coloured with brown marker

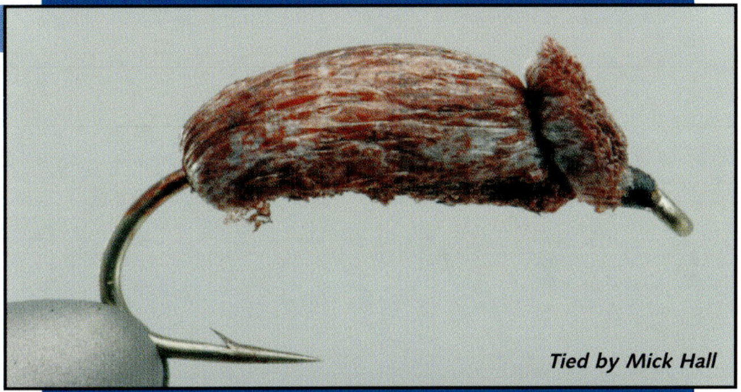

Tied by Mick Hall

STYX SPECIAL

HOOK: Kamasan B401, size 8–12
THREAD: Black
TAIL: Furnace hackle tips
BODY: Black cock hackle, palmered and trimmed
RIB: Gold wire
HACKLE: Furnace cock

Tied by Michael Milczuk

TEA TREE BEETLE

HOOK: Kamasan B401, size 10–14
THREAD: Black
BODY: Black seal's fur
BACK: Light brown raffia
HACKLE: Black cock

Tied by Michael Milczuk

TEA TREE BEETLE BROWN

HOOK: Kamasan B401, size 10–14
TAG: Fluoro white floss
THREAD: Black
BODY: Light brown dry fly dubbing
BACK: Light brown raffia
HACKLE: Brown cock

Tied by Peter Coulson

TEA TREE BEETLE TURKEY BROW

HOOK: Kamasan B401, size 10–14
THREAD: Black
BODY: Dark brown deer hair, spun and clipped
WING: Brown turkey
HACKLE: Brown cock

Tied by Peter Coulson

TROTHODG

HOOK: Kamasan B401, size 12–16
THREAD: Dark brown 8/0
BODY: Peacock herl
LEGS: Three or four golden pheasant tippets on each side
MIDDLE HACKLE: Black cock hackle
THORAX: Peacock herl
FRONT HACKLE: Black and furnace hackles, interwound

Tied by Ezra Bibby

Fish this to places where you think fish may be holding—alongside logs, through bubble-lines and around rocks. You can also sit it in front of cruising fish.

WHITE TAG

HOOK: Dry fly, size 14–18
THREAD: Black 6/0
TAG: Fluoro white floss
BODY: Peacock herl
HACKLE: Brown cock

Tied by Peter Coulson

This fly is for the fish that get sick of the Red Tag.

YELLOW LADYBIRD

HOOK: Dry fly, size 14–18
THREAD: Black 6/0
UNDERBODY: Burnt orange synthetic dubbing.
OVERBODY: Yellow closed cell foam with black dots from waterproof marker
HEAD: Black thread

Tied by Peter Coulson

FOAM BUTT BEETLE

HOOK: Kamasan B401, size 12–14
THREAD: Black
TAG & UNDERBODY: Black closed cell foam
BODY: Peacock herl
HACKLE: Black hen

This pattern floats all day.

Tied by Peter Coulson

MINI CHRISTMAS BEETLE

HOOK: Dry fly, size 14–18
THREAD: Black
BODY: Peacock herl
BACK: Pearl Shell Back
LEGS: Black cock
HEAD: Black

This is best fished down and across.

Tied by Peter Coulson

BLACK BEETLE 2

HOOK: Kamasan B401, size 12–14
THREAD: Black
TAG: Red Uni-Yarn
BODY: Peacock herl
HACKLE: Brown or black hen
FEELERS: Pheasant tail
BACK: Black Evasote (dry fly foam)

Tied by David Dodd

CHAPTER 2

CADDIS ADULTS

ANDY'S CADDIS

HOOK: Down-eye dry fly, size 16–18
THREAD: Black waxed mono cord
BODY: Four turkey tail fibres
WING: Turkey feather fibres
HACKLE: Black cock
WING: Light elk hair tied on top of hook. Allow several fibres to spin along the sides. The wing butts forward of the hook eye are trimmed off to form the head.

This is a useful fly for quiet pools and lakes, also good for fish focussed on small food items.

Tied by Andrew Lines

BUCKTAIL CADDIS

HOOK: Long shank dry fly, size 8–18
THREAD: Yellow 8/0
BODY: Orange floss
HACKLE: Red cock, palmered along body
WING: Brown bucktail

Tied by Michael Milczuk

C.D.C. GOLD CADDIS

HOOK: Kamasan B170, size 10–16
THREAD: Black
BODY: Dubbed green Antron
WING: Three yellow C.D.C. feathers, laid flat
HEAD: Black

This fly works well in all caddis hatches regardless of the shape, colour and size of the naturals

Tied by Peter Coulson

C.D.C. SKATER

HOOK: Dry fly, size 10–14
THREAD: Tan 6/0
BODY: Dark brown hare's ear
RIB: Flat gold tinsel
HACKLE: C.D.C. feathers, brown
COLLAR: Olive deer hair
HEAD: Dark brown hare's ear

This is the fly you would fish when it is too dark to see but the fish are still rising. Cast downstream and skate the fly around. This will normally result in a strike. Wait for the line to tighten up.

Tied by Adam Royter

Tied by Matt Wales

E-Z SNOWFLAKE

HOOK: Kamasan B170, size 10–16
THREAD: White
BODY: Dubbed natural C.D.C.
WING: Five C.D.C. feathers laid flat
THORAX: Dubbed C.D.C.
ANTENNAE: Two grey MicroFiBetts

Tied by David Dodd

ELK HAIR CADDIS

HOOK: Kamasan B401, size 12–18
THREAD: Black
BODY: Dubbed brown or olive
RIB: Fine silver wire
HACKLE: Red or fiery brown, palmered
WING: Light elk hair tied on top of hook. Allow several fibres to spin along the sides. The wing butts forward of the hook eye are trimmed off to form the head.

Fish this fly when caddis are hatching or dancing on the water. This is also a great attractor fly in summer because it can represent a hopper.

Tied by Laurie Ellul

ELLUL CADDIS

HOOK: Dry fly, size 12–18
THREAD: Black
BODY: Dubbed to suit natural
WING: Mustad Fantastic Wing, trimmed to shape and coloured with permanent markers
ANTENNAE: Stripped hackle stems
LEGS: Cock hackle, tied beard style

Tie by Adam Royter

GRAYLING CADDIS

HOOK: Dry fly, size 14–18
THREAD: Tan 6/0
BODY: Ultra fine dry fly, light green
UNDERWING: C.D.C. natural or light blue dun
OVERWING: Elk hair

This fly is a good all-rounder. Originally designed for the small mouth of the grayling it works well on trout. This fly can be fished in the afternoon to a good caddis hatch and in the smaller sizes it makes a good skating caddis.

MUSTARD CADDIS

HOOK: Kamasan B400, size 12
THREAD: 6/0 grey
BODY: Bright green Antron dubbing and palmered white cock hackle
WING: Light elk and mustard organza wing colour with grey marker

This low profile fly sits in the surface film and gives a good representation of the natural. It's also buoyant enough to be fished in fast water and is excellent in daytime hatches.

Tied by Adam Royter

REES CADDIS

HOOK: Size 12–16 dry fly
THREAD: White
BODY: Lime green Antron dubbing
WING: Natural deer hair
HACKLE: White cock hackle
ANTENNAE: Stripped white cock hackle

Fished with a greased leader the angler can twitch, jerk or skate the fly to entice the fish to take. Rising trout in impoundments will often sip the fly down gently.

Tied by Stuart Rees

SNOWFLAKE CADDIS

HOOK: Kamasan B170, size 10–16
THREAD: White
BODY: Dubbed white C.D.C.
WING: Three white C.D.C. feathers laid flat
THORAX: Dubbed C.D.C.
ANTENNAE: Two white C.D.C. stems

Tied by Peter Coulson

SNOWFLAKE CADDIS YARRA

HOOK: Kamasan B170, size 10–16
THREAD: White
BODY: Dubbed natural C.D.C.
WING: Three white C.D.C. feathers laid flat
THORAX: Dubbed C.D.C.
HEAD: Black

This is a great pattern to match the dancing snowflake caddis on the Yarra River in Victoria.

Tied by Peter Coulson

CHAPTER 3

CADDIS STICK & LARVAE

ANTRON STICK CADDIS

HOOK: Kamasan B175, size 10–14
THREAD: White
BODY: Lightly dubbed Antron colour to suit naturals
THORAX: Pure white thread
HACKLE: Ginger cock, third grade
HEAD: Off-white tying thread

Tied by Peter Coulson

B2 STICK CADDIS

HOOK: Tiemco 5212, size 12
THREAD: 6/0 brown
BODY: Brown Antron dubbing
HACKLE: Dark brown cock, palmered the full length of the body and clipped
HEAD: Yellow bucktail and dyed red pheasant tail

At one stage or another, every fly tier has tied their own stick caddis—this is one of my favourites. Primarily a lake caddis, it can also be used in the long slow pools of a river. A very slow retrieve is necessary.

Tied by Adam Royter

BEAD CADDIS GRUB

HOOK: Tiemco 2457, size 10–12
THREAD: Black
BODY: Five green, powder coated, brass beads
SHUCK: White poly yarn tied in behind the beads and pulled over
WING: Black hackle fibres
SIDE WINGS: Starling
THORAX: Peacock herl
HEAD: Black tying thread

Tied by Adam Royter

BURNT CADDIS

HOOK: Kamasan B830, size 8–12
THREAD: Black
TAIL: Black squirrel tail
BODY: Synthetic brown dubbing, burnt with lighter
LEGS: Black cock fibres
HEAD: Yellow floss

This fly works well in the western lakes of Victoria. It fishes best with a slow retrieve.

Tied by Peter Coulson

Tied by Peter Coulson

CADDIS EMERGER GREEN

HOOK: Dry fly, size 12–16
THREAD: Black 8/0
BUTT: White Antron, teased out
BODY: Lime green synthetic dubbing
RIB: Fine gold wire
THORAX: Peacock herl
HACKLE: Two turns of green partridge
HEAD: Black thread

This fly is best fished across and down at the start of a caddis hatch, raising the rod tip at the end of the swing.

Tied by David Dodd

CADDIS GRUB

HOOK: Tiemco 2457, size 10–12
THREAD: Black
BODY: Lightly dubbed, colour to suit naturals
RIB: Swannundaze fine, colour to suit naturals
THORAX: Black rabbit, picked out
WINGCASE: Black synthetic raffia
HEAD: Black tying thread

Tied by David Dodd

CADDIS GRUB BEAD HEAD

HOOK: Tiemco 2457, size 10–12
THREAD: Black
BODY: Lightly dubbed, colour to suit naturals
RIB: Swannundaze fine, colour to suit naturals
THORAX: Same as body, or peacock herl
HEAD: Medium gold bead

This fly is best when fished deep—nymphing style.

Tied by David Dodd

CADDIS PUPA BROWN

HOOK: Kamasan B175, size 12–16
THREAD: Black
BODY: Dubbed dark brown
RIB: Fine silver wire
LEGS: Beard style brown partridge
HEAD: Dark brown dubbing, lightly picked out

This fly can be fished on its own or in tandem with a Gold Bead Head Nymph, or under an Elk Hair Caddis during a hatch

CADDIS PUPA CREAM

HOOK: Kamasan B175, size 12–16
THREAD: Black
BODY: Dubbed cream
RIB: Fine silver wire
LEGS: Beard style brown partridge
HEAD: Dark brown dubbing, lightly picked out

This can be fished on its own or in tandem with a Gold Bead Head Nymph, or under an Elk Hair Caddis during a hatch

CADDIS PUPA GREY

HOOK: Kamasan B175, size 12–16
THREAD: Black
BODY: Dubbed dark grey
RIB: Fine silver wire
LEGS: Beard style brown partridge
HEAD: Dark brown dubbing, lightly picked out

This can be fished on its own or in tandem with a Gold Bead Head Nymph, or under an Elk Hair Caddis during a hatch

FLOSS CADDIS

HOOK: Tiemco 2457, size 10–12
THREAD: Black
BODY: Brown floss
LEGS: Pheasant tail
HEAD: Yellow floss

G B CADDIS

HOOK: Kamasan B 830, size 10–16
THREAD: Dark olive green
BODY: Ringneck pheasant tail barbs over-wrapped with dark olive thread
LEGS: Ringneck pheasant tail barbs
HEAD: Yellow thread

This fly is best fished slowly on a floating line in lakes.

Tied by Gerd Behneche

G B CADDIS GRUB

HOOK: Kamasan B175, size 12–14
THREAD: Black
BODY: Yellow seal's fur dubbing
RIB: Copper wire
THORAX: Fiery brown seal's fur dubbing
WINGCASE: Black crow
HACKLE: Brown cock
HEAD: Black tying thread

Tied by Adam Royter

GLASS CADDIS GRUB

HOOK: Tiemco 2457, size 10–12
THREAD: Black
BUTT: Light yellow Antron dubbing
BODY: Four green, glass beads
THORAX: Grey Antron, picked out
HEAD: Black tying thread

Tied by Adam Royter

GLASS CADDIS GRUB II

HOOK: Tiemco 2457, size 10–12
THREAD: Black
BODY: Five green, glass beads
SHUCK: White Antron tied in behind the beads and pulled over
WING: Black hackle fibres
SIDE WINGS: Starling
THORAX: Ostrich herl
HEAD: Black tying thread

Tied by Peter Coulson

GLASS & PARTRIDGE CADDIS

HOOK: Kamasan B401, size 10–14
THREAD: Olive
BUTT: Light yellow Antron dubbing
BODY: Four clear, glass beads
THORAX: Yellow Antron, picked out
HACKLE: Two turns of olive partridge
HEAD: Olive tying thread

This pattern is best fished down and across in rivers during a caddis hatch.

GOULBURN CADDIS

HOOK: Grub, size 8–14
THREAD: Black
BODY: Fine green dubbing
RIB: Copper wire
THORAX: Peacock herl
HEAD: Black tying thread

Tied by Muz Wilson

GRANT CADDIS

HOOK: Daiichi 1750, size 10–12
THREAD: Black
BODY: Orange and black Squirrel Blend dubbing, burnt
HACKLE: Grizzle
HEAD: Green fly line, singed

This fly is best fished slowly on a floating line in lakes.

Tied by Daryl Grant

GREEN CADDIS

HOOK: Dry fly, size 12–16
THREAD: Black 8/0
BODY: Lime green floss
THORAX: Fine black dubbing
WINGCASE: Pheasant tail pulled forward to create feelers
HEAD: Black thread

Tied by Adam Royter

GREEN GRUB

HOOK: Tiemco 2457, size 10–12
THREAD: Black
BUTT: Dark green Antron dubbing
BODY: Dark green Midge Lace
THORAX: Peacock herl
HEAD: Black tying thread

This is best fished upstream, nymphing style, under an Elk Hair Caddis.

Tied by Peter Coulson

JELLY CADDIS GRUB

Tied by Peter Coulson

HOOK: Tiemco 2457, size 10–12
THREAD: Black
BODY: Fluoro green soft plastic grub
SIDE WINGS: Clear plastic wing
THORAX: Black Antron, picked out
LEGS: Partridge breast feather
HEAD: Black tying thread

Fish this pattern down and across.

KIEWA CADDIS GRUB

Tied by Peter Coulson

HOOK: Tiemco 2457, size 12–14
THREAD: Black
BODY: Fine green Larva Lace
THORAX: Two turns of peacock herl
HEAD: Black tying thread

This pattern was originally tied for the Kiewa River in Victoria, but I have found it works everywhere.

LITTLE STICKY

Tied by Ezra Bibby

HOOK: B160, size 8–14
THREAD: White, colour with marker to suit dubbing
BODY EXTENSION: Stripped feather quill
BODY: Stripped peacock herl
HEAD & LEGS: Golden olive dubbing, teased out to form legs

MICK'S STICK CADDIS BLACK

Tied by Mick Hall

HOOK: Axisco dry 305, size 10–14
THREAD: Black
BODY: Floating fly line coloured black and brown with waterproof marker
LEGS: Three turns of brown ostrich herl
HEAD: Black tying thread

MICK'S STICK CADDIS OLIVE

HOOK: Axisco dry 305, size 10–14
THREAD: Olive
BODY: Floating fly line coloured black and brown with waterproof marker
LEGS: Three turns of olive ostrich herl
HEAD: Olive tying thread

Tied by Mick Hall

MODWARRIOR

HOOK: Kamasan B175, size 6–12
THREAD: White
TAIL: Black mink
BODY: Dubbed Scintilla peacock
HEAD: White floss

This fly is fished dead slowly along or near weedbeds representing a swimming stick caddis. Another excellent presentation is to attach a small strike indicator to the leader in order to suspend the fly at a required depth for extended periods.

Tied by Stuart Rees

PEACOCK & GOLD

HOOK: Kamasan B830, size 8–12
THREAD: Black
BODY: Peacock herl
HEAD: Gold wire

This fly is best fished deep and slowly.

Tied by Peter Coulson

PLAIT GRUB

HOOK: Tiemco 2457, size 10–12
THREAD: Black
BODY: Light olive floss under dark olive floss plaited
RIB: Fine copper wire
HEAD: Black tying thread

Tied by Peter Coulson

Tied by Peter Coulson

RABBIT CADDIS GRUB

HOOK: Kamasan B175, size 12–16
THREAD: Black 8/0
BODY: Dubbed natural rabbit, teased out
RIB: Fine gold wire
WING: Natural rabbit guard hairs
HEAD: Black thread

This is best fished across and down at the start of a caddis hatch, raising the rod tip at the end of the swing.

Tied by David Dodd

SCINTILLA STICK

HOOK: Tiemco 5262, size 12–14
THREAD: Yellow
BODY: Brown or olive Scintilla
THORAX: White wool
HACKLE: Soft hen
HEAD: Yellow tying thread
TYING NOTE: After dubbing Scintilla onto the hook, off. With a small flame heat the dubbing then mould it with fingers to the desired shape. Reattach the thread complete the fly.

Tied by David Dodd

SCINTILLA STICK BEAD HEAD

HOOK: Tiemco 5262, size 12–14
THREAD: Yellow
BODY: Brown or olive Scintilla
HACKLE: Golden Antron dubbing
HEAD: Yellow plastic bead
TYING NOTE: After dubbing Scintilla onto the hook, tie off. With a small flame heat the dubbing then mould it with fingers to the desired shape. Reattach the thread and complete the fly.

This fly is generally fished in tandem with a Gold Bead Head Nymph for river fishing.

Tied by David Dodd

STICK CADDIS

HOOK: Tiemco 5262, size 12–14
THREAD: Black
BODY: Peacock herl, sparsely dressed
HACKLE: Soft golden brown hen
HEAD: Yellow plastic bead

This fly is generally fished in tandem with a Gold Bead Head Nymph for river fishing.

STICK CADDIS

HOOK: Kamasan B 401, size 12–16
THREAD: Olive
BODY: Olive squirrel dubbing, trimmed
HEAD: Antron yarn, singed at tip
LEGS: Small bunch of hackle fibres, tied out over eye

Suspend this pattern under a dry fly, and set it as an ambush in likely areas.

Tied by Ezra Bibby

STICKY CADDIS

HOOK: Kamasan B175, size 10–16
THREAD: Yellow
TAIL: Double sided sticky tape rolled up in brown dubbing
BODY: Brown dubbing
LEGS: Brown cock
HEAD: Yellow dubbing

Tied by Muz Wilson

STICKY CADDIS BEADHEAD BROWN

HOOK: Kamasan B175, size 10–16
THREAD: Yellow
TAIL: Double sided sticky tape rolled up in brown dubbing
BODY: Brown dubbing
LEGS: Brown cock
HEAD: Yellow powder coated brass bead

Tied by Muz Wilson

STICKY CADDIS BEADHEAD GREEN

HOOK: Kamasan B175, size 10–16
THREAD: Yellow
TAIL: Double sided sticky tape rolled up in green dubbing
BODY: Green dubbing
LEGS: Brown cock
HEAD: Yellow powder coated brass bead

Tied by Muz Wilson

CHAPTER 4

DAMSELFLIES

BEAD EYE DAMSEL

HOOK: X-long B200, size 6–12
THREAD: Black 8/0
TAIL: Tan/Olive marabou
BODY: Olive wool palmered with olive cock hackle
TAG: Chartreuse egg yarn
RIB: Fine gold tinsel
EYES: Glass beads secured with tying thread and tinsel

Tied by Noel Jetson

BUTLER DAMSEL

HOOK: Dry fly extra long, size 10
THREAD: Black Uni-Thread 6/0
TAIL: Dark blue cock feather tip
BODY: Peacock herl
RIB: Fine gold wire
BODY HACKLE: Dark blue cock
HACKLE: Dark blue cock and tan cock

Tied by Roger Butler

DAMSEL IN DISTRESS

HOOK: TMC 200 R nymph, size 10–14
THREAD: Olive 6/0
RIBBING: Pearl Aurora thread and 1 kg nylon
TAIL: Olive marabou
LEGS: Green partridge
BODY: Mix 80% olive marabou to 20% lime Flashabou dubbing
WINGCASE: Pearl sheet
EYES: Burnt mono 20 kg

With lots of flash this damsel is a great pattern for discoloured water and in clear water works best when stripped fast.

Tied by Adam Royter

DAMSEL NYMPH (DODD)

HOOK: Kamasan B830, size 10–12
THREAD: Black
TAIL: Olive marabou
BODY: Olive dubbing
RIB: Copper wire
LEGS: Olive partridge
WINGCASE: Olive feather fibre
EYES: Black or brown made from the bristle of industrial broom, melted to a ball shape
THORAX: Dubbing same as body

Tied by David Dodd

DAMSEL NYMPH (RUMPF)

HOOK: Kamasan B820, size 12 slightly bent upwards in the middle
THREAD: Olive
TAIL: Dyed olive green partridge
RIB: Copper wire
BODY: Blend of Lazerlights and Litebrite dubbing
THORAX: Same as body with strands picked out to simulate legs
WINGCASE: Dyed olive pheasant tail
EYES: Spirit River small black plastic
HEAD: Black ostrich herl clipped

EXTENDED DAMSEL NYMPH

HOOK: Kamasan B175, size 10–12
THREAD: Black
TAIL: Olive Partridge threaded through clear Midge Tube
BODY: Olive dubbing
RIB: Copper wire
LEGS: Olive partridge
THORAX: Dubbing same as body
WINGCASE: Olive feather fibre
EYES: Black mono eyes, small

GIBSON'S DAMSEL NYMPH

HOOK: Kamasan B175, size 10–12
THREAD: Black
TAIL: Olive marabou
BODY: Olive brown dubbing
LEGS: Guinea fowl
WINGCASE: Scud Back, clear
EYES: Black mono eyes

GREEN DAMSEL NYMPH

HOOK: Kamasan B830, size 10–12
THREAD: Black
TAIL: Bright green marabou
BODY: Bright green mono cord
THORAX: Bright green dubbing
WINGCASE: Green raffia
EYES: Black mono eyes

JEANSIE'S DAMSEL

HOOK: Mustad, size 10–14
THREAD: Black
TAIL: Metallic craft thread twisted
BODY: Blue rabbit dubbing
WING: Grizzle hackle tips
HACKLE: Grizzle cut short
WINGCASE: Duck breast feather coloured with blue marker pen
EYES: Vinyl rib

This is best fished on cruising damsel feeders cast 2 m in front of and left for the fish to find.

Tied by Nick Jeans

JEANSIE'S DAMSEL 2

HOOK: Mustad, size 10–14
THREAD: Black
TAIL: Metallic craft thread twisted
BODY: Black seal's fur
WING: Grizzle hackle tips
EYES: Vinyl rib
HACKLE: Blue grizzle cut top and bottom

This is best fished on cruising damsel feeders cast 2 m in front of and left for the fish to find. Mark 2 floats better than the original, so suits broken water.

Tied by Nick Jeans

JEANSIE'S DAMSEL NYMPH

HOOK: Mustad, size 10–14
THREAD: Olive green
TAIL: Olive green marabou overbound with tying thread
BODY: Olive green Antron
LEGS: Olive green partridge
WINGCASE: Olive green partridge
EYES: Vinyl Rib

Tied by Nick Jeans

MARABOU DAMSEL

HOOK: TMC 200, size 10–14
THREAD: Green
TAIL: Olive marabou
BODY: Butts from tail, palmered
RIB: Pearl Krystal Flash
LEGS: Olive partridge
WINGCASE: Olive feather fibre
EYES: Burnt monofilament
THORAX: Chopped marabou and green Flashabou mixed and dubbed
THORAX COVER: Pearl Mylar

Tied by Laurie Ellul

Tied by Mick hall

MICK'S DAMSEL

HOOK: Wet fly, size 10–14
THREAD: Olive 6/0
TAIL: Dark olive marabou
BODY: Dark olive green rabbit
EYES: Dark olive plastic beads tied on with 3 kg mono through the holes of the beads

Tied by Peter Coulson

OLIVE DAMSEL

HOOK: Kamasan B830, size 10–12
THREAD: Black
TAIL: Olive marabou
BODY: Olive marabou dubbing
RIB: Fine pearl tinsel
LEGS: Olive partridge
WINGCASE: Pearl sheet
EYES: Small brass beads tied on with wire
THORAX: Olive marabou dubbing

Tied by Peter Coulson

PETE'S DAMSEL

HOOK: Kamasan B175, size 10–12
THREAD: Olive
TAIL: Olive and tan marabou
BODY: Olive and tan marabou dubbing
HACKLE: Brown cock
WINGCASE: Peacock herl
THORAX: Dubbing same as body
HEAD: Black

Tied by Adam Royter

POLAR DAMSEL

HOOK: Black Magic A 10–14
THREAD: Olive 6/0
TAIL: Chartreuse Polar Fibre and Hoffman Soft Hackle olive
LEGS: Hoffman Soft Hackle olive
WINGCASE: Comes Alive root beer
BODY: Polar Fibre chartreuse dubbing
EYES: 10 kg burnt nylon

This is a very lightweight fly that excels in shallow water. The Polar Fibre gives great movement with a strip tease retrieve.

RABBIT DAMSEL NYMPH

HOOK: Kamasan B 830, size 10–12
THREAD: Black
TAIL: Rabbit dyed olive (Dylon 34 and a quarter of a teaspoon of fiery brown)
BODY: Dubbing same as tail
RIB: Copper wire
LEGS: Fiery brown partridge
WINGCASE: Dark olive feather fibre
EYES: Black or brown made from the bristle of industrial broom, melted to a ball shape
THORAX: Dubbing same as body

Tied by David Dodd

ROGER BOOTH DAMSEL

HOOK: Kamasan B175, size 12–14
THREAD: Olive 6/0
TAIL: Dark olive rabbit
BODY: Dark olive green rabbit
EYES: Black plastic beads on a mono post

Tied by Roger Booth

STICKY DAMSEL NYMPH

HOOK: Kamasan B175, size 10–14
THREAD: Black
TAIL: Olive marabou rolled up in double-sided tape
BODY: Olive dubbing
WINGCASE: Olive feather fibre
THORAX: Olive dubbing
EYES: Burnt mono

Tied by Muz Wilson

THE VET

HOOK: Kamasan B830, size 12
THREAD: Yellow
TAIL: Olive green marabou
BODY: Mix of olive green seal's fur and Antron
RIB: Fine gold Lure Flash
HEAD: Peacock herl

This fly is best fished in lakes during winter and spring on a floating line. The retrieve should be very short and fast.

Tied by Vic Howlett

CHAPTER 5

D R I E S

ADAMS WULFF

HOOK: Dry fly, size 8–16
THREAD: Tan
TAIL: Natural deer hair
BODY: Grey muskrat dubbing
RIB: Tying thread
HACKLE: Brown and grizzle interwound
WING: White calf tail, tied upright and divided

Tied by Jack Dennis

AUSABLE WULFF

HOOK: Dry fly, size 8–16
THREAD: Red
TAIL: Natural deer hair
BODY: Tan dubbing
HACKLE: Grizzle or cree cock hackle
WING: White calf tail, tied upright and divided

Tied by Jack Dennis

BIBIO HOPPER

HOOK: Tiemco 102Y, size 11–13
THREAD: Black, waxed
BODY: Claret seal's fur black, red, black
RIB: Pearl tinsel
LEGS: Dyed red pheasant tippets tied in so that they are below the perpendicular
HACKLE: Black, three turns of grade 2 or 3
HEAD: Black thread

This is a magic fly. Always put it on the point with an Orange Carrot in the middle and a claret Bob's Bits on top. Give it a good tug along as well.

Tied by Neil Grose

BOB'S BITS

HOOK: Tiemco 102Y, size 13–15
THREAD: Black or brown
BODY: Red seal's fur, tied slim
HACKLE: Soft brown or black grade 3 or 4 with 2–3 turns
HEAD: Fluoro thread

This fly is best tied onto the top dropper position on the leader above the Carrot, and about 1.5 m from the fly line. Smaller sizes are good when midges are up, or when the water becomes glassy calm.

Tied by Neil Grose

Tied by Jack Dennis

BWO PARA WULFF

HOOK: Dry fly, size 10–16
THREAD: Grey
TAIL: Grey cock hackle fibres, tied divided
BODY: Grey beaver dubbing
RIB: Fine pearl Flashabou
HACKLE: Grey cock hackle, tied parachute style
WING: White calf body hair tied upright and divided

Tied by Laurie Ellul

BREAD FLY

HOOK: Wide gape dry fly, size 10–14
THREAD: White
TAIL: Red fox or squirrel
BODY: Alternating bands of white deer hair and white marabou, trimmed roughly

Tied by Peter Coulson

BREAD FLY 2

HOOK: Dry fly, size 10–14
THREAD: White
BODY: Alternating bands of white and tan deer hair and white and cream marabou, trimmed

Tied by Neil Grose

CLARET CARROT

HOOK: Tiemco 102Y, size 11–13
THREAD: Brown, waxed
BODY: Claret seal's fur dubbed rough
HACKLE: Fiery brown cock 3–4 turns
HEAD: Fluoro pink thread

This fly is best fished in the middle of a three fly leader, and fished with movement.

CLARET DAPPER

HOOK: Tiemco 102Y, size 11–13
THREAD: Brown, waxed
TAIL: Pheasant tail
BODY: Claret seal's fur dubbed rough
RIB: Silver oval tinsel
HACKLE: Mallard, laid back
HEAD: Brown thread

Tied by Neil Grose

COCH-Y-BONDDU

HOOK: Dry fly, size 10–16
THREAD: Black
TAG: Gold tinsel or wire
BODY: Peacock herl
HACKLE: Furnace cock

Tied by Michael Milczuk

GREENWELL'S GLORY

HOOK: Mustad R30, size 16
THREAD: Freshly waxed Pearsall's Gossamer PGST 3 (pale 'primrose' yellow)
TAILS: Light coch-y-bonddu or furnace
BODY: The tying silk
RIB: Fine gold wire
WINGS: Hen blackbird secondary, or any medium grey quill
HACKLE: Light coch-y-bonddu or furnace

Tied by Rick Keam

GREY DRAKE PARA WULFF

HOOK: Dry fly, size 8–16
THREAD: Black
TAIL: Grey hackle fibres tied divided
BODY: Grey muskrat dubbing
RIB: Fine pearl Flashabou
HACKLE: Grizzle cock hackle, parachute style
WING: White calf tail tied upright and divided

Tied by Jack Dennis

GREY DUSTER

Tied by Michael Milczuk

HOOK: Dry fly, size 10–16
THREAD: Black
BODY: Dubbed rabbit fur
HACKLE: Badger cock hackle

HAIRWING COACHMAN

Tied by Michael Milczuk

HOOK: Dry fly, size 14–20
THREAD: Black
TAIL: Golden pheasant tippets
BODY: Peacock herl
WING: White bucktail
HACKLE: Furnace, two wraps only

HEATHER

Tied by Andrew Lines

HOOK: Offset point dry fly, size 10–14
THREAD: Yellow monochord
TAIL: Deer hair
BODY: Hot orange seal's fur or substitute
RIB: Clear 1 kg mono
HACKLE: Honey dun or very light red game

This is mainly a small stream fly, ideal as an indicator that still works when waterlogged and submerged.

LITTLE RED ROOSTER

Tied by Adam Royter

HOOK: Kamasan B400, size 18
THREAD: Tan 8/0
BODY: Uni-Flex red and peacock herl
WING: Poly yarn tied crosswise
THORAX: Super Fine black

This is my favourite autumn dry fly for small waters. Just when the last of the caddis hatches are on and the tiny dun comes out fish this fly to the rises during the day.

ORANGE CARROT

HOOK: Tiemco 102Y, size 11–13
THREAD: Brown, waxed
BODY: Orange seal's fur dubbed rough
HACKLE: Orange grizzle cock 3–4 turns
HEAD: Fluoro pink thread

This fly is best fished in the middle of a three fly leader, and fished with movement.

Tied by Neil Grose

PALE STIMULATOR

HOOK: Kamasan B180, size 8–12
THREAD: White
TAIL: Pale deer or elk hair
BODY: White seal's fur palmered with grizzle cock hackle
RIB: Fine gold wire
UNDERWING: Pale deer or elk hair
OVERWING: Krystal Flash
THORAX & HEAD: White seal's fur palmered-with grizzle cock hackle

This pattern floats very well and is ideal for suspending a bead head nymph.

Tied by Ezra Bibby

PARACHUTE ADAMS

HOOK: Dry fly, size 10–16
THREAD: White
TAIL: Brown and grizzle cock hackle fibres
BODY: Muskrat underfur
WING: Calf body hair
HACKLE: Grizzle and brown cock hackle, interwound

This pattern floats very well and is ideal for suspending a bead head nymph.

Tied by Ezra Bibby

PMD PARA WULFF

HOOK: Dry fly, size 10–16
THREAD: Black
TAIL: Brown cock hackle fibres
BODY: Grey dubbing
RIB: Fine pearl Flashabou
HACKLE: Grey cock hackle, tied parachute style
WING: Tan deer hair, tied upright and divided

Tied by Jack Dennis

Tied by Peter Coulson

POSSUM WULFF

HOOK: Kamasan B401, size 10–16
THREAD: Olive green
TAIL: Blue dun hackle fibres
BODY: Cream synthetic dubbing
RIB: Fine gold wire
HACKLE: Blue dun cock
WING: Natural possum fur, tied upright and divided

This is a good late summer fly on the Mitta Mitta River.

Tied by Michael Milczuk

RAT FACED McDOUGAL

HOOK: Dry fly, size 10–14
THREAD: Black
BODY: Grey deer hair, spun and clipped
HACKLE: Black cock hackle

Tied by Jack Dennis

ROYAL HUMPY

HOOK: Dry fly, size 8–16
THREAD: Red
TAIL: Dark brown deer hair
BODY: Red silk
BACK: Light deer hair
HACKLE: Fiery brown cock hackle
WING: White calf tail tied upright and divided

Tied by Jack Dennis

ROYAL HUMPY-OLIVE

HOOK: Dry fly, size 8–16
THREAD: Olive
TAIL: Dark brown deer hair
BODY: Green dubbing
BACK: Olive deer hair
HACKLE: Cree cock hackle
WING: White calf tail, tied upright and divided

ROYAL WULFF

HOOK: Kamasan B401, size 10–16
THREAD: Black
TAIL: Natural deer hair or moose hair
BODY: Peacock herl with a red floss centre band
HACKLE: Brown cock
WING: White calf tail, tied upright and divided

This is a world famous attractor dry fly.

Tied by David Dodd

ROYTER SPECIAL

HOOK: Dry fly, size 10–18
THREAD: Tan 6/0
HACKLE: Grizzle cock tied palmer style
BODY: Light green Antron dubbing
OVERWING: Black duck breast feathers
HEAD HACKLE: Brown and tan cock

This fly is designed to be fished when more than one insect is hatching at a time—caddis and duns. A good choppy water fly, it is also useful in holding up a nymph in a dropper rig.

Tied by Adam Royter

THE YARRA FLY

HOOK: Tiemco 200, size 18–24
THREAD: Olive green
BODY: Olive green rabbit dubbing
RIB: Pearl Krystal Flash
WING: White C.D.C.
LEGS: Moose

Tied by Daryl Grant

ZULU (Variation)

HOOK: Kamasan B405, size 12–16
THREAD: Black
TAIL: Red wool
BODY: Black seal's fur palmered with black hackle
RIB: Fine silver wire
HEAD HACKLE: Black cock

This is a good general purpose fly, and is extremely effective in smaller sizes during a rise of chironomid midges.

Tied by David Dodd

CHAPTER 6

DUNS

A.B.O.B.

HOOK: Up eye grub hook, size 10–14
TAIL: Hackle fibres
RIB: Fine copper wire
NYMPH BODY: Possum fur
DUN BODY: Hen saddle feather cut to shape
POST: HIVIS
HACKLE: Brown saddle, parachute style

Tied By Muz Wilson

ADAMS

HOOK: Kamasan B401, size 10–20
THREAD: Brown or grey
TAIL: Brown and grizzle hackle fibres mixed
BODY: Muskrat or medium grey poly dubbing
WING: Grizzle hackle tips tied upright and divided
HACKLE: Brown and grizzle cock mixed

Tied by David Dodd

ASH DUN

HOOK: Kamasan B405, size 10–14
THREAD: Black
TAIL: Chocolate dun cock hackle fibres
BODY: Stripped peacock herl
THORAX: Dark brown super fine dubbing
WINGS: Matched pair of mallard duck quills
HACKLE: Chocolate dun cock

Tied by Ashley Artis

ASH DUN NO HACKLE

HOOK: Kamasan B405, size 10–14
THREAD: Black
TAIL: Chocolate dun cock hackle fibres, divided
BODY: Stripped peacock herl
THORAX: Dark brown super fine dubbing
WINGS: Matched pair of mallard duck quills

Tied by Ashley Artis

Tied by Michael Milczuk

ATALOPHLEBIA DUN

HOOK: Kamasan B401, size 12–16
THREAD: Black
TAIL: Dun hackle fibres
BODY: Blue dun hackle, palmered over tying thread
WING: Turkey quill slip
HACKLE: Blue dun and brown, interwound

Tied by Adam Royter

BIG YARRA DUN

HOOK: Kamasan B400, size 10–12
THREAD: Black 6/0
TAIL: Moose hair
BODY: Ginger rabbit dubbing
HACKLE: Light ginger cock

Unfortunately the hatch of duns that inspired this fly lasts for only a few weeks, but when it is on you'll know all about it!

Tied by Bruce Gibson

BRETT WOLF PARA DUN

HOOK: Tiemco 100, size 10–14
THREAD: Black
TAIL: Chocolate dun cock hackle fibres
BODY: Red brown possum dubbing
RIB: Black Uni-floss
WINGS: Dark C.D.C.
HACKLE: Grizzle brown cock, parachute style

Tied by Peter Coulson

BROWN TWILIGHT BEAUTY

HOOK: Kamasan B401, size 10–14
THREAD: Brown
TAIL: Chocolate dun cock hackle fibres
BODY: Fine dark brown dubbing
THORAX: Dark brown Super Fine dubbing
WINGS: Matched pair of dark brown quills
HACKLE: Chocolate dun cock

CHOCOLATE PARA DUN

HOOK: Partridge, size 12–14
THREAD: Black
TAIL: Chocolate cock hackle fibres
BODY: Red brown seal's fur dubbing
RIB: Fine copper wire
WINGS: Brown HIVIS
HACKLE: Chocolate brown cock, parachute style

Tied by Peter Coulson

CHURCH WINDOW DUN

HOOK: Kamasan B405, size 10–12
THREAD: Black
TAIL: Pheasant tail
BODY: Fine brown synthetic dubbing
WINGS: Matched pair church window feathers
HACKLE: Ginger cock clipped off at the bottom

Tied by Adam Royter

DARK DUN

HOOK: Tiemco 100, size 12
THREAD: Black
TAIL: Black cock hackle fibres
BODY: Natural possum dubbing
WINGS: Fine hare hair
HACKLE: Black cock parachute style

Tied by Bruce Gibson

FUNNELDUN

HOOK: Up eye dry fly, size 12–20
THREAD: To suit thorax colour
TAIL: Hackle fibres or guard hairs, twice as long as hook
BODY: Fine dubbing, colour to suit natural
HACKLE: Oversized cock hackle, swept forward when winding the thorax
THORAX: Fine dubbing, slightly darker than body

Designed to float hook-bend up. To facilitate this, cut a 45 degree 'vee' from the top centre of the hackle.

Tied by Ezra Bibby

BOGONG BEAUTY

HOOK: Kamasan B401, size 10–14
THREAD: Black
TAIL: Large bunch of grizzle hackle fibres
BODY: Grey fur from the scrub possum
RIB: Gold twist or wire
HACKLE: Grizzle tied full and heavy

This pattern works best fished upstream along the side of runs or broken water. The fly is dressed full to ride high in rough water.

HAIR WING DUN

HOOK: Kamasan B401, size 10–14
THREAD: Brown or black
TAIL: Medium dun hackle fibres
BODY: Dark brown dyed possum dubbing
WING: Natural deer hair tied upright
HACKLE: Medium to dark dun clipped to form a 'V' on the underside to assist the fly's stability.

HAIR WING KOSCIUSZKO DUN

HOOK: Kamasan B401, size 10–12
THREAD: Brown
TAIL: Rhode Island Red, tied long
BODY: Rusty possum dubbing
WING: Natural deer hair tied upright and divided
HACKLE: Rhode Island Red clipped to form a 'V' on the underside to assist the fly's stability.

HEMAROYTER SPECIAL

HOOK: Dry fly, size 12–14
THREAD: Black 6/0
TAIL: Pheasant tail fibres, natural
BODY: Pheasant tail fibres natural
WING: C.D.C. brown
HACKLE: Dyed brown cock

This fly was developed to imitate a small, dark brown dun that hatches in great number on dams and a small lake near my home. In larger sizes this fly has proven its value in the Central Highlands of Tasmania.

HIVIS DUN

HOOK: Kamasan B401, size 12–14
THREAD: Brown
TAIL: Dark dun hackle fibres
BODY: Dark brown mink
WING: HIVIS wing coated with Flexcement and pressed flat after tying in. Cut and trim when dry
HACKLE: Dark dun

A useful fly when trout become keyed into the upright winged stage of the hatching dun, especially during the drying out phase prior to flight.

Tied by David Dodd

LOOP WING DUN

HOOK: B401, size 12–16
THREAD: Brown
TAIL: Furnace hackle fibres
BODY: Chocolate brown dry fly dubbing, taken under hackle
RIB: Fine copper wire
HACKLE: Furnace cock, trimmed under
WING: Pheasant tail fibres, looped

Tied by Ezra Bibby

KOSCIUSZKO DUN

HOOK: Dry fly, size 8–12
THREAD: Light Cahill
TAIL: Buff hackle fibres
BODY: Camel dubbing, buff
WING: Buff hackle points
HACKLE: Buff

Tied by Michael Milczuk

KOSCIUSZKO DUN WILSON

HOOK: TMC 100, size 8–12
THREAD: Black
HEAD: Tying silk
TAIL: Tan bucktail
BODY: Sparkle dubbing
WING: Light ginger hen hackle tips
FIRST HACKLE: Oversized light ginger rooster
SECOND HACKLE: Undersized olive grizzle

Tied by Muz Wilson

Tied by Peter Coulson

LOWRIDER PARA DUN

HOOK: Tiemco, size 10–14
THREAD: Black
TAIL: Chocolate dun cock hackle fibres
BODY: Red brown dubbing mix
RIB: Fine copper wire
POST: Dubbing ball of brown Antron
HACKLE: Brown cock parachute style

Tied by Peter Coulson

MITTA DUN

HOOK: Kamasan B440, size 12–16
THREAD: Black
TAIL: Natural black cock hackle fibres
BODY: Grey rabbit underfur
RIB: Fine green wire
HACKLE: Dyed charcoal grizzle cock

This fly was developed on north-east Victoria's Mitta Mitta River and is best fished in late summer, on dark and dirty afternoons.

Tied by Ezra Bibby

OCTOBER DUN

HOOK: Dry fly, size 12–14
THREAD: Black
TAIL: Mallard duck fibres
BODY: Red seal's fur and rabbit in mixed colours
WINGS: Matched pair of mallard duck quills
HACKLE: Light brown cock

Tied by Bruce Gibson

PARA DUN

HOOK: Tiemco 100, size 14
THREAD: Black
TAIL: Chocolate dun cock hackle fibres
BODY: Natural possum and dark rabbit dubbing
RIB: Fine silver wire
WINGS: Craft wool
HACKLE: Grizzle brown cock, parachute style

PARACHUTE DUN

HOOK: Kamasan 405, size 12–16
THREAD: Grey thread
TAIL: Cream hackle fibres
BODY: Dun sparkle dubbing
POST: White and white HIVIS
HACKLE: Tan saddle

Tied by Muz Wilson

PARACHUTE DUN BROWN

HOOK: Kamasan 405, size 12–16
THREAD: Black thread
TAIL: Brown hackle fibres
BODY: Brown sparkle dubbing
POST: Brown and white HIVIS
HACKLE: Brown saddle

Tied by Muz Wilson

PEACOCK DUN

HOOK: Up eye dry, size 12–16
THREAD: White, coloured with marker to suit dubbing
TAIL: Moose hair
BODY EXTENSION: Stripped feather quill
BODY: Stripped peacock herl
THORAX: Tiewell 'peacock' dubbing
HACKLE: Dark dun, parachute
WING/POST: HIVIS

Tied by Ezra Bibby

PECK'S DUN

HOOK: Kamasan B 401, size 12–16
THREAD: Brown
TAIL: Chocolate or furnace hackle fibres
BODY: Tying silk
BODY HACKLE: Small brown or grizzle cock hackle
WING: Turkey wing slip, folded
HACKLE: Brown, grizzle or furnace

Tied by Ezra Bibby

QUILL DUN

Tied by Peter Coulson

HOOK: Tiemco 100, size 12–16
THREAD: Black
TAIL: Ash dun cock hackle fibres
BODY: Stripped peacock herl
THORAX: Fine tan dubbing
HACKLE: Ginger brown cock

QUILL GORDON

Tied by Michael Milczuk

HOOK: Kamasan B 401, size 12–16
THREAD: Black
TAIL: Mallard flank fibres
BODY: Stripped peacock herl
RIB: Extra fine copper wire
WING: Mallard flank fibres
HACKLE: Dark dun

SHAVING BRUSH

Tied by David Dodd

HOOK: Dry fly, size 10–14
THREAD: Black
TAIL: Black cock hackle fibres
BODY: Dark dubbing mix
RIB: Copper wire
WINGS: Natural deer hair angled steeply forward
HEAD: Brown dubbing ball to flare out the deer hair

THORAX DUN CREAM

Tied by Muz Wilson

HOOK: Dry fly hook, size 12–16
TAIL: Dun hackle fibres widely split by dubbing ball
BODY: Cream Super Fine dubbing
WING: Dun turkey fibres
HACKLE: Saddle hackle, trimmed underneath

THORAX DUN TAN

HOOK: Dry fly hook, size 12–16
TAIL: Tan hackle fibres widely split by dubbing ball
BODY: Dark dun Super Fine dubbing
WING: Tan turkey fibres
HACKLE: Saddle hackle, trimmed underneath

Tied by Muz Wilson

THREADPOST DUN

HOOK: Dry fly, size 10–14
THREAD: Black
TAIL: Tan cock hackle fibres
BODY: Fine dark dubbing
THORAX: Dark brown fine dubbing
HACKLE: Grizzle cock
TYING NOTES: The hackle is tied parachute style around a post of looped tying thread, then wrapped.

Tied by David Dodd

TURKEY DUN

HOOK: Kamasan B405, size 10–14
THREAD: Black
TAIL: Mix of black and brown cock hackle fibres
BODY: Brown thread
BODY HACKLE: Ginger cock
WINGS: Matched pair of turkey quills
HACKLE: Two turns of brown and three turns of grizzle cock

Tied by Peter Coulson

TWILIGHT BEAUTY

HOOK: Kamasan B405, size 10–14
THREAD: Black
TAIL: Chocolate dun cock hackle fibres
BODY: Black thread
THORAX: Black thread
WINGS: Matched pair of starling quills
HACKLE: Chocolate dun cock

This fly has to be the best pattern to fish at twilight after a hatch.

Tied by Peter Coulson

CHAPTER 7

EMERGERS

C.D.C. EMERGER

HOOK: Kamasan B401, size 12–14
THREAD: Brown
TAIL: Red cock hackle fibres
BODY: Dark dun dubbing
RIB: Fine copper wire
THORAX: Hare's ear, picked out
WINGCASE: C.D.C. grey
TYING NOTE: When forming the wingcase ensure that a space is created between the thorax and the Cul de Canard feathers, enabling the fly to trap air during casting and thus aiding floatability.

Tied by David Dodd

C.D.C. EMERGER-COULSON

HOOK: Tiemco, size 10–14
THREAD: Black
TAIL: Partridge fibres
BODY: Natural rabbit
WING: Natural C.D.C.
HEAD: Black tying thread

This fly is good for stillwater hatches.

Tied by Peter Coulson

C.D.C. EMERGER-ROYTER

HOOK: Kamasan B401, size 12–14
THREAD: Black
TAIL: Red cock hackle fibres
BODY: Olive rabbit and Antron dubbing mix
RIB: Fine gold wire
THORAX: Olive rabbit and Antron dubbing mix
WINGCASE & WING: C.D.C. red brown

Tied by Adam Royter

DEERHAIR EMERGER

HOOK: Kamasan B100, size 12–18
THREAD: Brown
BODY: Hare's mask dubbing
RIB: Brown tying silk
WING: Medium to fine deer hair

Tied by Ezra Bibby

Tied by Adam Royter

DEERHAIR EMERGER-ROYTER

HOOK: Kamasan B100, size 10–14
THREAD: Black
TAIL: Red cock hackle fibres
BODY: Dark seal's fur dubbing mix
RIB: Gold tinsel
WING: Medium to fine deer hair tied in as a wing and clipped off short
HEAD: Black tying thread

Tied by Adam Royter

FOAM EMERGER

HOOK: Kamasan B100, size 10–14
THREAD: Black
TAIL: Red cock hackle fibres
BODY: Dark seal's fur dubbing mix
WING: Black foam tied in as a wing and clipped off short
HEAD: Black tying thread

This emerger will float all day.

Tied by Adam Royter

FOAM EMERGER 2

HOOK: Tiemco 200R, size 10–14
THREAD: Black
TAIL: Tan hackle fibres
BODY: Brown Antron dubbing mix
RIB: Gold tinsel
THORAX: Closed cell foam coloured with waterproof marker
HEAD: Black tying thread

Tied by Peter Coulson

FOAM BACK EMERGER

HOOK: Tiemco, size 10–14
THREAD: Black
TAIL: Partridge fibres
BODY: Natural rabbit
WING: White closed cell foam cut short
HACKLE: Light tan cock hackle two sizes smaller than normal
HEAD: Yellow tying thread

FOAM BACK EMERGER 2

HOOK: Partridge, size 10–14
THREAD: Black
TAIL: Partridge fibres
BODY: Natural rabbit
WINGCASE: Tan closed cell foam
HACKLE: Light tan cock hackle
HEAD: Black tying thread
TYING NOTE: Tie the foam in as a post and wrap the hackle around it parachute style then pull the foam over to create a wing case and tie it off at the head.

FOAM HEAD EMERGER

HOOK: Tiemco, size 10–14
THREAD: Black
TAIL: Partridge fibres
BODY: Natural rabbit picked out
RIB: Gold tinsel
HEAD: White closed cell foam

This fly is great for fast water. It hangs below the surface and you can easily see the white foam head.

HIGHLAND EMERGER

HOOK: Kamasan B401, size 10–14
THREAD: Black or brown
TAIL: Dark dun cock
BODY: Dark brown dubbing
HACKLE: Dark dun wound over thorax
WING: Feather fibre coated with Flexcement, when dry cut to shape

Cast to rising fish or drift crosswind with a nymph dropper during a dun hatch.

HIGH-VIS EMERGER

HOOK: Kamasan B100–10, size 8–16
THREAD: 6/0 black
TAIL: Pheasant tail fibres
RIBBING: copper wire
BODY: Pheasant tail fibres wrapped
THORAX: Dark brown Antron dubbing
HACKLE: Cock hackle dyed dark brown
WING: Mustard organza wing

When fishing an emerger it is hard to see at the best of times. This pattern incorporates a highly visible wing on the top that stands out.

NELSON GREEN EMERGER

HOOK: Kamasan B100 (or B100G), size 12–16
THREAD: 8/0
TAIL: Furnace hackle fibres
BODY: Light green nymph dubbing
THORAX: Olive nymph dubbing
THORAX COVER: Tan or green closed cell foam
HACKLE: Furnace cock hackle tied parachute style around the thorax cover then swept back as the foam is pulled forward.
RIB: Fine gold wire

KLINKHAMER SPECIAL

HOOK: Kamasan B100, size 8–18
THREAD: 8/0 for body, Spiderweb for hackle
BODY: Tan dubbing
HACKLE: Natural (or blue) dun, parachute style
WING/POST: HIVIS

PACKAGE EMERGER

HOOK: Kamasan B100, size 10–14
THREAD: Black
TAIL: Red cock hackle fibres
BODY: Brown seal's fur dubbing mix
RIB: Gold wire
WING: Packaging from photo negative tied in as a wing and clipped off short
HACKLE: Ginger cock clipped flat at the bottom
HEAD: Black tying thread

Best fished on stillwater with a long leader

PARTRIDGE EMERGER

HOOK: Kamasan B401, size 10–14
THREAD: Black or brown
TAIL: Dark brown cock
BODY: Dark brown dubbing
WING: Partridge breast feather
HACKLE: Dark brown clipped at the bottom

Cast to rising fish or drift crosswind during dun hatch.

POSSUM EMERGER

HOOK: Tiemco 102Y, size 10–14
THREAD: Brown Uni-Thread 6/0
TAIL: Dark brown possum fibres 4–5 mm long
RIB: Dull copper wire
BODY: Dark brown possum fur
WING: Dark brown possum fur tied in a loop to form a wing

In the early part of the hatch apply floatant to the wing bud portion. Once the hatch swings into gear waterproof the whole fly and give it good firm pulls.

Tied by Neil Grose

SCURVY DOG

HOOK: Dry, size 10
THREAD: Tan 6/0
TAIL: Pheasant tail
BODY DUBBING: Brown rabbit 90% and white Antron 10%
HACKLE: Dyed dark brown cock
THORAX DUBBING: Dark brown Antron

This is a good fly when the fish are going on emergers. One of my favourite Tasmanian flies.

Tied by Adam Royter

SPARKLE EMERGER

HOOK: Kamasan B100G, size 10–14
THREAD: White
BODY: Masterbright golden olive dubbing
HACKLE: Furnace cock, thorax style
RIB: Fine gold wire
WING: Caribou hair

This fly fishes well as a dropper behind an Elk Hair Caddis. It is also good to throw at fish rising in quiet corners.

Tied by Ezra Bibby

SPLIT TAIL EMERGER

HOOK: Kamasan B401, size 10–14
THREAD: Black or brown
TAIL: Two pheasant tail fibres, split by dubbing ball
BODY: Dark brown Antron dubbing
RIB: Fine black nylon
WING: Partridge breast feather
HACKLE: Dark brown clipped at the bottom

Tied by Adam Royter

CHAPTER 8

HOPPERS

ADAM'S HOPPER

HOOK: Dry fly, size 10–16
THREAD: Tan
BODY: Yellow deer hair tied in at butt and pulled forward
WING: Turkey feather
LEGS: Fine, red cock hackle tips
HEAD & COLLAR: Yellow deer hair under and natural deer hair on top, flared and clipped

Tied by Adam Royter

BADJA HOPPER #1

HOOK: Dry fly, size 14–16
THREAD: Brown
TAIL: Yellow hackle tip
BODY: Tying thread, palmered with a Cree cock hackle

Use this fly early in the hopper season.

Tied by Michael Milczuk

BADJA HOPPER #2

HOOK: Long shank dry fly, size 12–14
THREAD: Black
TAIL: Yellow hackle tip
BODY: Peacock herl
UNDERWING: Yellow hackle tip
OVERWING: Deer hair
HACKLE: Cree cock hackle

This fly is for the middle of the hopper season.

Tied by Michael Milczuk

BADJA HOPPER #3

HOOK: Long shank dry fly, size 6–12
THREAD: Black
TAIL: Pink wool
BODY: Off-white wool
RIB: Green tinsel
UNDERWING: Yellow hackle tip
OVERWING: Deer hair
LEGS: Golden pheasant tail fibres
HACKLE: Brown

This pattern is for late in the hopper season.

Tied by Michael Milczuk

Tied by Michael Milczuk

BANJO'S HOPPER

HOOK: Dry fly, size 10–14
THREAD: Black
TAG: Red wool
BODY: Deer hair, spun and clipped
WING: Golden pheasant tippets
LEGS: Pheasant tail fibres, knotted
HEAD: Deer hair, spun and clipped

Tied by Peter Coulson

BERCHDOLT'S HOPPER

HOOK: Dry fly, size 8–16
THREAD: Black
TAIL: Golden pheasant tippets
BODY: Green floss
RIB: Yellow floss
WING: Pheasant breast feather
HACKLE: Orange cock and golden pheasant tippets

Tied by Peter Coulson

BULLET HEAD HOPPER

HOOK: Kamasan B401, size 10–12
THREAD: Black 3/0 mono
BODY: Green Antron dubbing
LEGS: Pheasant tippets tied each side
WING: Light coloured turkey feather
OVERWING: Olive deer hair
HEAD: Olive deer hair tied bullet style

Tied by Adam Royter

CASUAL HOPPER

HOOK: Dry fly, size 8–12
THREAD: Black
TAIL: Small bunch of fine red tinsel
BODY: Tan Krystal Flash chenille
UNDERWING: Comes Alive root beer
OVERWING: Deer hair
HEAD: Deer hair, spun and clipped

CHOOK STIMULATOR

HOOK: Dry fly 2X long, size 6–10
THREAD: Red
TAIL: Natural deer hair
BODY: Peacock herl
BODY HACKLE: Grizzle
WING: Natural deer hair
THORAX: Yellow Antron dubbing
HACKLE: Grizzle
HEAD: Red

Tied: Michael Milczuk

THE CORK

HOOK: Long shank, size 10–12
THREAD: Yellow
BODY: Cork
RIB: Yellow thread

Though it doesn't represent anything in particular, this old north English lure works well on fast, broken water.

Tied by Peter Coulson

CURRANGO HOPPER

HOOK: Partridge dry fly, size 10–14
THREAD: Brown
TAIL: Golden pheasant tippets
BODY: Olive floss
RIB: Condor herl (substitute with peacock herl)
LEGS: Golden pheasant tippets
WING: Duck breast feather, wonderwing fashion
HACKLE: Furnace, with partridge in front

Tied by Michael Milczuk

DEER HAIR HOPPER

HOOK: Long shank size, 8–12
THREAD: Yellow
TAIL & WING: Natural deer hair
HEAD: Deer hair, spun and clipped

Tied by Peter Coulson

Tied by Peter Coulson

DROWNED HOPPER

HOOK: Kamasan B175, size 6–10
THREAD: Black 3/0
BODY: Mottled grey rabbit dubbing
HACKLE: Wood duck wing feather
HEAD: Mottled grey rabbit and peacock herl dubbing

This fly is best fished down and across fast water on hot windy days. It suites the small rivers of north-eastern Victoria.

Tied by Edgewater

EDGEWATER RUBBER LEG HOPPE

HOOK: Long shank, size 8–12
THREAD: Yellow
BODY & HEAD: Yellow foam
WING: Natural turkey
LEGS: Yellow rubber

Tied by Peter Coulson

FLASH SIMULATOR

HOOK: Dry fly 2X long, size 6–10
THREAD: Hot pink
TAIL: Natural deer hair
BODY: Pearl Microflash
BODY HACKLE: Ginger cock
WING: Natural deer hair and pearl Microflash
THORAX: Burgundy dubbing
HACKLE: Ginger cock
HEAD: Hot pink thread

This fly is best fished with a nymph as a dropper.

Tied by Peter Coulson

FOAM HOPPER

HOOK: Dry fly, size 10–14
THREAD: Yellow
BODY & HEAD: Tan foam
RIB: Yellow thread
LEGS: Orange rubber
HACKLE: Ginger cock

DAVE'S HOPPER

HOOK: Long shank, size 8–12
THREAD: Yellow
TAIL: Red deer hair under yellow wool
BODY: Yellow wool
RIB: Fiery red hackle, clipped
WING: Brown turkey feather
LEGS: Six to eight pheasant tail fibres, knotted
COLLAR: Olive deer hair
HEAD: Olive deer hair, spun and clipped

Tied by Fulling Mill

GERRY'S HOPPER

HOOK: Long shank, size 8–10
THREAD: Black
TAIL: Golden pheasant tippets
BODY: Yellow chenille
LEGS: Five golden pheasant tippets each side
WING: Primary feather from turkey wing
HEAD: Deer hair, spun and clipped

Tied by Gerry Karsten

GLEN INNES HOPPER II

HOOK: Dry fly, size 12–16
THREAD: Black 8/0
BODY: Yellow chenille
WING: Two grizzle and two red hackle tips
HACKLE: Grizzle cock

Tied by Peter Coulson

GLEN INNES HOPPER

HOOK: Dry fly, size 8–12
THREAD: Black
TAIL: Grizzle hackle fibres
BODY: Yellow and brown chenille
RIB: Fine gold wire
UNDERWING: Scarlet hackle tips
OVERWING: Grizzle hackle tips
HACKLE: Grizzle

Tied by Michael Milczuk

Tied by Peter Coulson

GOULBURN STIMULATOR

HOOK: Dry fly 2X long, size 6–10
THREAD: Red
TAIL: Natural deer hair
BODY: Yellow yarn
BODY HACKLE: Rhode Island Red cock
WING: Natural deer hair
THORAX: Orange Antron dubbing
HACKLE: Grizzle

This fly is best fished with a nymph as a dropper.

Tied by Peter Coulson

GREEN LEGGED HOPPER

HOOK: Dry fly, size 6–10
THREAD: Black
BODY: Green closed cell foam, cut to shape
LEGS: Green raffia
WING: Natural dark brown deer hair
HEAD: Natural deer hair tied in bullet style

Tied by Mick Hall

HALL'S HOPPER

HOOK: Dry fly long shank, size 6–12
THREAD: Light tan 6/0, waxed
BODY: Latex mayfly body
LEGS: Small bunch of golden pheasant tippets tied in each side
HEAD: Deer hair tied muddler style

Tied by Michael Milczuk

HI FLOATER HOPPER

HOOK: Dry fly, size 6–12
THREAD: Tan 6/0
BODY & HEAD: Yellow round closed cell foam
WING: Turkey feather
LEGS: Tan Krystal Flash, knotted
HACKLE: Ginger brown cock

HOPPER

HOOK: Kamasan B401, size 10–12
THREAD: Yellow 3/0 mono
BODY: Yellow lure foam
LEGS: Synthetic raffia knotted
UNDERWING: Red feather from cock pheasant
OVERWING: Deer hair
HEAD: Deer hair tied bullet style

Tied by David Dodd

HOPPER HACKLE

HOOK: Dry fly long shank, size 8–12
THREAD: Orange 6/0 waxed
TAIL: Claret cock fibres
BODY: Natural raffia over fine grey dubbing
HACKLE: Partridge over golden pheasant
HEAD: Orange thread

This is an excellent old pattern that can be fished wet or dry.

Tied by Peter Coulson

JAMES HOPPER

HOOK: Dry fly, size 8–12
BODY: Yellow closed cell foam trimmed to shape
HEAD & WING: Deer hair tied bullet head fashion
LEGS: Knotted yellow rubber legs and antennae

Tied by James Hill

JOE'S HOPPER

HOOK: Long shank, size 8–12
THREAD: Black
TAIL: Red deer hair under yellow foam
BODY: Yellow foam
RIB: Fiery red hackle, clipped
SIDE WINGS: Brown turkey feather
HACKLE: Grizzle and brown cock

Tied by Fulling Mill

Tied by Fulling Mill

JOE'S WOOL HOPPER

HOOK: Long shank, size 8–12
THREAD: Black
TAIL: Red deer hair under lemon wool
BODY: Lemon wool
RIB: Fiery red hackle, clipped
SIDE WINGS: Brown turkey feather
HACKLE: Grizzle and brown cock

Tied by Rick Keam

KEAM'S POLYHOPPER

HOOK: 2X short shank, size 10
THREAD: White 3/0 mono
BODY: Lemon or pale yellowish cream closed cell foam
LEGS: Knotted yellow waterproof raffia highlighted with green or brown marking pen
HEAD/THORAX/ FORELEGS/ WING: Deer hair tied 'Keam Collar' style

Tied by Rick Keam

KEAM'S AUTUMN HOPPER

HOOK: 2X short shank, size 12
THREAD: White 3/0 mono
BODY: Creamish white closed cell foam
LEGS: Knotted tan waterproof raffia highlighted with orange marking pen
HEAD/ THORAX/ FORELEGS/ WING: Deer hair tied 'Keam Collar' style

Tied by Daryl Grant

MADAM MOUNTAIN HOPPER

HOOK: Kamasan B 405, size 12
THREAD: Black
TAIL: Natural deer hair
BODY: Brown olive SLF dubbing
HEAD & WING: Deer hair tied bullet head fashion
LEGS: Green floating fly line tied Madam X style

MURRINDINDI MAULER

HOOK: Dry fly, size 10–16
THREAD: Yellow
BODY: Yellow deer hair tied in at butt and pulled forward
WING: Turkey feather
LEGS: Red pheasant tail, knotted
HEAD & COLLAR: Yellow under and lime green deer hair on top, flared and clipped

This fly works well on hot afternoons on the Murrindindi River in Victoria.

Tied by Peter Coulson

NOEL'S NOBBY HOPPER

HOOK: Dry fly, size 12–16
THREAD: Tan
BODY: Yellow chenille
WING: Golden pheasant tippets under natural deer hair
HEAD: Natural deer hair, spun and clipped

Tied by Peter Coulson

RED LEG POLY HOPPER

HOOK: Kamasan B401, size 10–12
THREAD: Yellow 3/0 mono
BODY: Lemon lure foam
LEGS: Orange synthetic raffia, knotted and coloured with red marking pen
WING: Yellow raffia under turkey feather
OVERWING: Deer hair
HEAD: Olive and tan deer hair tied bullet style

Tied by Peter Coulson

RUBBER LEGS

HOOK: 3X Long shank, size 8–12
THREAD: Yellow
BUTT: Red deer hair
BODY: Yellow foam 2 mm, cut 6 mm wide
BODY HACKLE: Brown cock hackle
UNDERWING & POST: Calf tail
OVERWING: Brown turkey quill
LEGS: Round rubber, knotted and clipped
HEAD & COLLAR: Deer hair tied bullet style
HACKLE: Grizzle cock hackle tied parachute style

Tied by Laurie Ellul

Tied by Peter Coulson

SNOWY MOUNTAINS HOPPER

HOOK: Dry fly, size 10–16
THREAD: Black 6/0
TAIL: Golden pheasant crest
BODY: Yellow floss
RID: Fine copper wire
WING: Yellow breast feather with black tips
HEAD HACKLE: Partridge breast feather overlaid with golden pheasant tips

Tied by Peter Coulson

THE BREDBO

HOOK: Kamasan B175, size 8–14
THREAD: Orange 6/0 waxed
BODY: Orange floss
RIB: Oval gold tinsel
WING: Golden pheasant tippets tied long under barbe brown hen wing feather
HACKLE: Brown partridge, swept back
HEAD: Orange thread

This is a great wet pattern representing drowned hoppers. Fish this fly do and across when hoppers are on the water.

Tied by Peter Coulson

T C

HOOK: Dry fly, size 10–14
THREAD: Black
BODY: Natural unwashed wool
RIB: Black thread
UNDERWING: Duck breast feather
OVERWING: Black deer hair
HEAD: Black deer hair, spun and clipped

This fly works very well at Lake Eucumbene when hoppers are on the water.

Tied by Murray Wilson

WILSON HOPPER

HOOK: Dry fly, size 10–12
THREAD: Dark brown
BODY: Yellow foam, shaped
UNDERWING: Brown turkey feather
HEAD & OVERWING: Deer hair tied bullet style

FLASH JACK

HOOK: Tiemco 2312, size 6
THREAD: White 3/0 mono
BODY: Buff coloured closed cell foam
LEGS: Tam waterproof raffia highlighted with marker pens
UNDERWING: Yellow raffia highlighted with black marker
OVERWING: Dark turkey or Tasmanian wallaby
HEAD, THORAX & FORELEGS: Single large bunch of deer hair tied Keam Collar-style
TYING NOTE: Body length should be 35 mm excluding legs

Tied by Rick Keam

CHAPTER 9

MATUKAS

BLACK MATUKA

HOOK: Medium length, size 8–12
THREAD: Black
BODY: Black Antron blend
RIB: Fine red wire
WING: Three black hen feathers
HEAD: Black

Tied by Michael Milczuk

COCKEYE MATUKU

HOOK: Kamasan B175, size 6–10
THREAD: Black
BODY: Dark olive seal's fur
RIB: Fine gold wire
WING: Three dark olive grizzle hen feathers
HACKLE: Two turns of dark olive grizzle hen feather
CHEEKS: Jungle cock

Best fished on a floating line with a short sharp retrieve.

Tied by Peter Coulson

GALAXIA FLUORO GREEN

HOOK: X-long B200, size 4–10
THREAD: Black 6/0
WING: 4 yellow and black saddle hackles, matuka style
BODY: Fluoro green chenille
RIB: Flat silver tinsel followed by oval silver tinsel
THROAT: Red wool
HEAD: Build up with thread and lacquer
CHEEKS: Pearl Flashabou (short)

Tied by Noel Jetson

GALAXIA GRIZZLE

HOOK: X-long B200, size 4–10
THREAD: Black 6/0
WING: 4–6 brown grizzle saddle hackles
BODY: Brown chenille
RIB: Flat silver tinsel followed by oval silver tinsel
TAG: Pearl Flashabou
THROAT: Brown grizzle hackle fibres
HEAD: Build up with thread and lacquer
EYE: Painted yellow with black pupil
TOPPING: Pearl Flashabou (short)

Tied by Noel Jetson

Tied by Noel Jetson

GALAXIA OLIVE

HOOK: X-long B200, size 4–10
THREAD: Red 6/0
WING: 4–6 olive saddle hackles, matuka style
BODY: Olive wool
RIB: Fine copper wire
THROAT: Pearl Flashabou
HEAD: Red thread varnished

Tied by Noel Jetson

GALAXIA WHITEBAIT

HOOK: X-long B200, size 4–10
THREAD: Yellow 6/0
WING: 4–6 Cree saddle hackles, matuka style
BODY: Silver Flashabou
RIB: Fine oval silver tinsel
THROAT: Red hackle fibres
HEAD: Tying thread varnished

Tied by Michael Milczuk

GREEN MATUKA

HOOK: Medium length, size 8–12
THREAD: Black
BODY: Green Antron blend
RIB: Fine gold wire
WING: Three dark, centred hen feathers
HEAD: Black

Tied by Peter Coulson

GREY MATUKA

HOOK: Kamasan B175, size 6–10
THREAD: Black
BODY: Grey seal's fur
RIB: Oval silver tinsel
WING: Two grey grizzle hen feathers

Good for flooded lake margins for smelting fish. Fish on a floating line with a long leader.

HORROR

HOOK: 2X long, size 4–10
THREAD: Black
BODY: Dark brown chenille
RIB: Silver wire
WING: Three dark, centred hen feathers or badger
HACKLE: Brown cock tied in palmer style
CHEEKS: Jungle cock
HEAD: Black

JUNO MATUKA

HOOK: X-long B200, size 4–10
THREAD: Pearsall's black silk
WING: 4–6 black hen hackles, matuka style
BODY: Front half black seal's fur, rear half red seal's fur dubbing
RIB: Flat silver tinsel followed by oval silver tinsel
CHEEKS: Jungle cock
HEAD: Tying thread varnished

LITTLE BROWN MATUKA

HOOK: Kamasan B175, size 10–16
THREAD: Black
BODY: Dark brown seal's fur
RIB: Fine gold wire
WING: Three brown hen feathers
HACKLE: Two turns of brown hen feather

BLACK & RED MATUKA

HOOK: Long shank wet, size 12–6
THREAD: Black
BODY: Red chenille
RIB: Gold wire
WING: Three black hen feathers
HEAD: Tying thread

MINI MATUKA

Tied by Peter Coulson

HOOK: Kamasan B175, size 12–16
THREAD: Black
BODY: Dark olive seal's fur
RIB: Fine gold wire
WING: Three dark olive grizzle hen feathers
HACKLE: Two turns of dark olive grizzle hen feather

This is best fished on a floating line with short, sharp retrieves. This fly regularly catches large browns in both rivers and lakes.

PETER'S GLORY

Tied by Peter Coulson

HOOK: Kamasan B175, size 8–12
THREAD: Black
BODY: Orange seal's fur
RIB: Fine gold wire
WING: Three orange grizzle hen feathers
HACKLE: Two turns of orange grizzle hen feather

This is best fished on floating line with short, sharp and erratic retrieves. This fly fishes best in rivers leading into winter.

RED & BLACK MATUKA (variation

Tied by Peter Coulson

HOOK: Kamasan B175, size 12–16
THREAD: Black
BODY: Dark red seal's fur
RIB: Fine gold wire
WING: Three black grizzle hen feathers
HACKLE: Two turns of dark olive grizzle hen feather

RED THROAT WHITEBAIT

Tied by Noel Jetson

HOOK: X-long wet fly limerick, size 4–10
THREAD: Black 6/0
WING: Cree cock hackles, matuka style
BODY: Grey wool dubbing
RIB: Flat silver tinsel
THROAT: Red hackle fibres

SIDE-ON MATUKA

HOOK: Kamasan B175, size 8–12
THREAD: Red
BODY: Off-white dubbing blend
RIB: Flat gold tinsel
WING: Three grey hen feathers tied down on their side
HEAD: Red

This pattern swims with a lot of movement. Slow to medium retrieves work best. It also works well on smelting fish.

Tied by Peter Coulson

SORELL GALAXIA

HOOK: X-long B200, size 4–8
THREAD: Black 6/0
WING: 4–6 furnace saddle hackles, matuka style
BODY: Yellow chenille
RIB: Flat silver tinsel followed by oval silver tinsel
THROAT: Red hackle fibres
HEAD: Build up with thread and lacquer
TAG: Red floss

Tied by Noel Jetson

THE WHITEBAIT FLY

HOOK: Wet fly, size 8–12
THREAD: Black
BODY: Dirty white seal's fur
RIB: Fine black wire
WING: Three light ginger grizzle feathers
HEAD: Lemon tying thread

Tied by Paul Adama

WIGRAM'S ROBIN

HOOK: Tiemco 9300, size 8
BUTT: Fluorescent red wool
BODY: Black seal's fur dubbing
RIB: Gold twist or copper wire
WING: Four black hen feathers, tightly ribbed over the black dubbing so they cock slightly upwards, prevently them fouling the bend
CHEEKS: Two jungle cock feathers

Best fished to worm feeders in the shallows and around the rocky edges of lakes when trout are feeding on smelt.

Tied by David Dodd

CHAPTER 10

MIDGE DRIES & SUSPENDERS

BADGER MIDGE BALL

HOOK: Dry fly hook, size 12
THREAD: Black 8/0
BODY: Badger cock hackle wound tightly along the whole of the hook shank

Place the fly near feeding trout when midges are balling up.

Tied by Rick Keam

BALLING MIDGE

HOOK: Kamasan B 401, size 12–14
THREAD: Black 8/0
BODY: Black cock hackle wound tightly along the whole of the hook shank and trimmed to a ball

Place the fly near feeding trout or when midges are balling up.

Tied by Mick Hall

C.D.C. MIDGE

HOOK: Kamasan B 160, size 12–16
THREAD: Black
TAIL: Tuft of white Antron body wool
BODY: Floss—colour to suit
RIB: Fine silver wire
THORAX: Peacock herl
WINGCASE: C.D.C. tied over thorax, shuttlecock style

Just prior to hatching, a midge hangs in the surface film motionless. The C.D.C. feathers enable the fly to hang in the film but also enable the fly angler to see the fly.

Tied by David Dodd

C.D.C. SUSPENDER BUZZER

HOOK: Kamasan B 160, size 12–20
THREAD: Black
BODY: Dubbing-colour to suit
RIB: Fine silver wire
THORAX: Dubbing—colour to suit
WINGCASE: C.D.C. tied over thorax, shuttlecock style

Just prior to hatching, a midge hangs in the surface film motionless. The C.D.C. feathers enable the fly to hang in the film but also enable the fly angler to see the fly.

Tied by David Dodd

Tied by Ezra Bibby

CONVIVIAL CHIRONOMID

HOOK: Kamasan B 100, size 12–20
THREAD: Black
BODY: Grey dubbing, scruffy
WINGS: Starling wing tips
HACKLE: Grizzle cock, one or two turns

Tied by Adam Royter

GLOW GNAT

HOOK: Dry fly hook, size 12–18
THREAD: Black or brown
BODY: Glow in the dark tape
HACKLE: Grizzle tied palmer style along shank

Tied by Peter Coulson

GREY SEDGE

HOOK: Dry fly hook, size 10–16
THREAD: Yellow
HACKLE: Grizzle, tied palmer style along shank
WING: A single grizzle hackle tip

This pattern works well on lakes with a ripple on them. Try skating the fly every now and then.

Tied by David Dodd

GRIFFITHS GNAT

HOOK: Dry fly hook, size 12–18
THREAD: Black or brown
BODY: Peacock herl
HACKLE: Grizzle, tied palmer style along shank

This fly is effective during a hatch of chironomid and when adult midges ball up.

LEIGH'S MIDGE

HOOK: Dry fly hook, size 14
THREAD: Black 8/0
BODY: Furnace cock hackle tied palmer along shank, with white cock hackle intertwined

Retrieve the fly across the surface with sharp, 5 cm strips. It works during a hatch, or as a searching pattern and is primarily a lake fly.

Tied by Bill Ricketts

MATING MIDGE

HOOK: Kamasan B 401, size 14–12
THREAD: Black 8/0
BODY: Pale green dubbing
HACKLE: Grizzle cock hackle, tied fore and aft

Cast this fly close to feeding fish and twitch it slightly.

Tied by Mick Hall

MIDGE BALL

HOOK: Tiemco 102Y, size 15–19
THREAD: Black
HACKLE: Grizzle, tied palmer style along shank and trim bottom points of hackle flat

Tied by David Dodd

RICKETTS CHIRONOMID

HOOK: Size 12–14
THREAD: Pearsall's olive tying silk
BODY: Pearsall's olive tying silk
RIB: Yellow tying silk
LEGS: Two turns of soft badger hackle, stripped on one side and wound so it slopes back
WINGCASE: Black hackle fibres

Fish this fly with a steady, slow retrieve as an emerging pupae.

Tied by Rick Keam

Tied by Rick Keam

SURFACE HANGING MIDGE

HOOK: Dry fly, size 12–16
THREAD: Black 8/0
BODY: Tying silk
RIB: Yellow tying silk
HACKLE: Black cock hackle

Tied by Rick Keam

SURFACE HANGING MIDGE (variati

HOOK: Dry fly, size 12–16
THREAD: Black 8/0
BODY: Tying silk
RIB: Yellow tying silk
HACKLE: Black cock hackle, separated with figure-of-eight wraps

Tied by Mick Hall

THE FULL STOP

HOOK: Kamasan B 401, size 18–20
THREAD: Black 8/0
BODY: Grizzle cock hackle tied full and clipped to form a round ball about 4 or 5 mm in diameter

Drift his fly along bubble and current lines when adult midges are balling to mate.

Tied by Peter Coulson

HALO MIDGE EMERGER

HOOK: Kamasan B160, size 12–16
THREAD: Black
BODY: Seal's fur mix
RIB: Fine pearl tinsel
THORAX: White closed cell foam
SPIKE: Orange deer hair

C.D.C. MIDGE SHUCK

HOOK: Kamasan B175, size 12–16
THREAD: Tan
BODY: Tan C.D.C. dubbed in and picked out

Tied by Peter Coulson

MOSSIE

HOOK: Kamasan B175, size 10–16
THREAD: Black
TAIL: White Antron
BODY: Grey thread
RIB: Black thread
THORAX: Fine black dubbing
WING: Grey C.D.C.
GILLS: White Antron

Tied by Peter Coulson

BLACK CHIRONOMID II

HOOK: Kamasan B175, size 16–20
THREAD: Black
BODY: Black thread
RIB: Fine silver wire
THORAX: Black seal's fur dubbing
GILLS: White Antron

This is a great pattern for Lake Eucumbene.

Tied by Peter Coulson

BROWN CHIRONOMID

HOOK: Kamasan B175, size 16–20
THREAD: Brown
BODY: Brown thread
RIB: Fine silver wire
THORAX: Brown seal's fur dubbing
GILLS: White Antron

This is a great pattern for Lake Eucumbene.

Tied by Peter Coulson

CHAPTER 11

MIDGE LARVAE & PUPAE

BEADHEAD BLOODWORM

HOOK: Kamasan B175, size 10–14
THREAD: Red
BODY: Red chenille
HEAD: Small brass bead

Tied by Adam Royter

BEADHEAD CHIRONOMID

HOOK: Kamasan B175, size 10–14
THREAD: White
TAIL: White Poly Yarn
BODY: Holographic tinsel
THORAX: Grey Antron dubbing
GILLS: White Poly Yarn
HEAD: Clear glass bead

Tied by Adam Royter

BLACK CHIRONOMID

HOOK: Midge size 18
THREAD: Black 8/0
BODY: Black floss
RIB: Fine copper wire
THORAX: Peacock herl
WING STUBS: Holographic tinsel
HEAD: Black thread, varnished

Fish this fly at dead drift on a long, fine, greased leader over rising fish. It can also be fished with a very slow retrieve or cast out and allowed to sink, before being retrieved in a long slow lift of the rod to simulate the midge rising to the surface. Takes can vary from soft and subtle to hard and savage.

Tied by Ian Mitchell

PEACOCK CHIRONOMID

HOOK: Kamasan B 175, size 16–20
THREAD: Black
BODY: Pheasant tail
THORAX: Peacock herl

Tied by Peter Coulson

BLOOD GRUB

HOOK: Grub, size 12–18
THREAD: Red
BODY: Red thread covered in epoxy

BLOOD MIDGE

HOOK: Kamasan B175, size 16–20
THREAD: Black
BODY: Red midge lace
THORAX: Red seal's fur dubbing
HEAD: Black tying thread

BLOODWORM

HOOK: Caddis grub hook size 12–14
THREAD: Red mono cord
BODY: Red reflective tape (available from automotive and safety equipment suppliers), lightly coat body with clear nail polish
HEAD: White Antron or baby wool

This is primarily a lake pattern. Retrieve the fly slowly with an occasional longer, faster strip to attract attention.

BLOODWORM NYMPH

HOOK: Kamasan B175, size 12–18
THREAD: Red
TAIL: Red marabou
BODY: Red thread
RIB: Fine red wire
HEAD: Red, powder coated, brass bead

This pattern is for getting down deep quickly.

RED TAG MIDGE

HOOK: Kamasan B175, size 16–20
THREAD: Black
TAIL: Red floss
BODY: Peacock herl
HEAD: Small brass bead

This is a great pattern for fishing where midges inhabit around the edges of current lines in slow pools.

BROWN PEARL CHIRONOMID

HOOK: Kamasan B175, size 10–16
THREAD: Brown
TAIL: White Antron
BODY: Brown dubbing mix
RIB: Fine pearl Sparkleflash
THORAX: Peacock herl
GILLS: White Antron

This pattern is best fished dead slowly.

BURGIS BLOODWORM

HOOK: Grub, size 10–14
THREAD: Red
TAIL: Red marabou
BODY: Red Crazy Lace
THORAX: Fine red wire
HEAD: Small brass bead

COPPER BEAD HARE'S EAR

HOOK: Kamasan B175, size 16–20
THREAD: Black
TAIL: Partridge breast feather fibres
BODY: Hare's ear dubbing, picked out
RIB: Fine copper wire
HEAD: Small 2 mm copper bead

This pattern is best fished in small, clear alpine lakes.

Tied by Adam Royter

CRYSTAL CHIRONOMID

HOOK: Kamasan B175, size 16–20
THREAD: Black
BODY: Light green Krystal Flash
THORAX: Peacock herl
HEAD: Black tying thread

Tied by David Embrey

DAM FLY

HOOK: Kamasan B175, size 10–20
THREAD: Black
TAIL: Black squirrel tail
BODY: Black thread
THORAX: Peacock herl
WING CASE: Black squirrel tail

This fly is best fished in dams on a floating line. The retrieve is relative to fly size—the smaller the fly, the slower the retrieve.

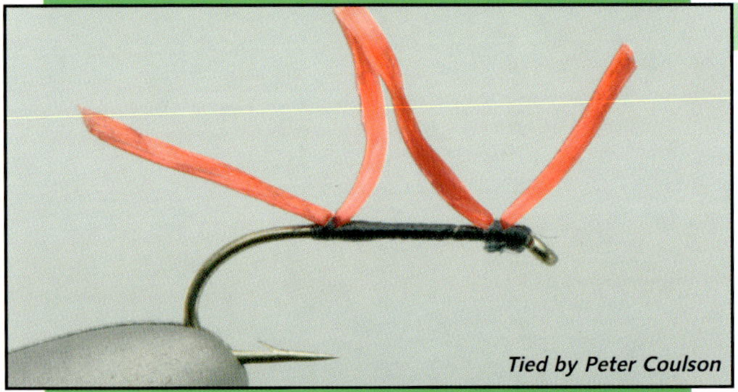

Tied by Peter Coulson

FLOSS BLOODWORM

HOOK: Kamasan B175, size 14–18
THREAD: Black
BODY: Red Flexi Floss

Cast the fly out and leave it.

Tied by Adam Royter

GLOW CHIRONOMID

HOOK: Kamasan B175, size 14–18
THREAD: Green
BODY: Green glow Sparkleflash
THORAX: Green Antron dubbing
GILLS: White foam

This fly works best as an attractor right on dark, when fish are still feeding on chironomid.

MIDGE CHIRONOMID

HOOK: Grub, size 12–18
THREAD: Black
BODY: Black thread
RIB: Fine silver Flashabou
BODY: Black thread
CHEEKS: Strip of orange floss
FINISH: Cover the whole fly in epoxy

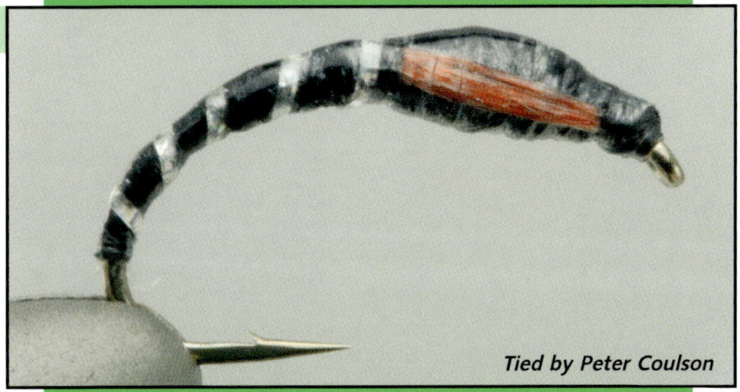

Tied by Peter Coulson

MIDGE CHIRONOMID II

HOOK: Grub, size 12–18
THREAD: Black
BODY: Grey thread
RIB: Black thread
BODY: Black thread
CHEEKS: Strip of red floss
FINISH: Cover the whole fly in epoxy

Tied by Peter Coulson

MIDGE PUPA

HOOK: Tiemco 102Y, size 15–19
THREAD: Black
BODY: Pearl tinsel wrapped in open turns allowing the black hook to show through
THORAX: Peacock herl
BREATHERS: White marabou

This fly may be fished alone, but is best fished under a midge ball.

Tied by David Dodd

MINI MIDGE

HOOK: Wet, size 18–22
THREAD: Black
BODY: Fine pearl Flashabou
THORAX: Black thread
SHUCK: White poly yarn

Tied by Adam Royter

CHAPTER 12

MUDDLERS

BLACK CROW MUDDLER

HOOK: Mustad 94841NPBR, size 4–10
THREAD: Black 6/0 Uni or Talon Strong thread
TAIL: Black crow
BODY: Gold tinsel
WING: Black crow
HEAD: Black deer hair, spun and clipped

This pattern is good on overcast days when fish are cruising the shallows mopping up and is best retrieved with a slow figure-of-eight.

Tied by Peter Coulson

BLACK MUDDLER

HOOK: Tiemco 9300, size 8–10
THREAD: Black
TAIL: Natural black squirrel tail
BODY: Silver tinsel
RIB: Silver wire
WING: Black crow
HEAD & COLLAR: Texas whitetail deer hair, black

This fly is generally fished after dark—black night, black fly. Fish the fly slowly along the surface with short jerks and the odd pause in between.

Tied by David Dodd

FLORRIE'S FLY

HOOK: Wilson dry fly salmon hook, size 8–12
THREAD: Black
BODY: Gold tinsel
UNDERWING: Brown deer hair
OVERWING: Black deer hair
HEAD: Black deer hair, spun and clipped

Tied by Michael Milczuk

FLUTTERING MUDDLER

HOOK: Mustad 94841NPBR, size 4–10
THREAD: Tan 6/0 Uni-Thread
BODY: Orange dubbing
RIB: Gold oval tinsel
WING & TAIL: Dyed orange turkey breast feathers or brown partridge, tied in matuka style
HEAD & COLLAR: Natural deer hair, spun and clipped

This is a great fly for when trout are feeding on young carp and redfin.

Tied by Peter Coulson

Tied by Ty Smith

JINDY MUDDLER

HOOK: Wet 2X long, size 8–12
THREAD: Black
TAIL: Black marabou
BODY: Gold oval tinsel
WING: Purple mallard and black marabou
OVERWING: Black deer hair
HEAD: Black deer hair, spun and clipped

Tied by Andrew Lions

LIONS MUDDLER

HOOK: Mustad 94841NPBR, size 4–10
THREAD: Black
TAG: Fluoro pink fabric paint
BODY: Silver Mylar tube
WING: Tan marabou with peacock herl on top
HEAD: Natural deer hair, spun and clipped
EYES: Fluoro yellow fabric paint

Tied by Keith Wiffen

WIFO'S MUDDLER

HOOK: Dry fly long, size 8
THREAD: Yellow
TAIL: Turkey quill wing, matched pair
BODY: Dubbed natural possum
HEAD & WING: Black deer hair, tied forward and pulled back over on top

This pattern was originally tied to fish the pools of the Kiewa River in Victoria at night. It is best fished down and across the slower water in small rivers at night.

Tied by Peter Coulson

ZONKER MUDDLER

HOOK: Mustad 94841NPBR, size 4–10
THREAD: Fluoro red
TAIL & BODY: Silver Mylar tube
WING: Grey rabbit Zonker strip
HEAD: Natural deer, hair spun and clipped

MUDDLER MINNOW

Tied by David Dodd

HOOK: Tiemco 9300, size 2–12
THREAD: Brown
TAIL: Mottled oak turkey
BODY: Gold tinsel
RIB: Gold wire
WING: Black or natural grey squirrel tail or two strips of mottled oak turkey
HEAD & COLLAR: Natural deer hair collar left surrounding the body and clipped to form head

Lighter coloured Muddlers are generally fished during moonlit nights. Fish the fly slowly along the surface with short jerks and the odd pause in-between. This fly can also be fished as a hopper during daylight hours.

MUDDLER SIMPSON

Tied by Peter Coulson

HOOK: Mustad 94841NPBR, size 4–10
THREAD: Black or olive 6/0 Uni or Talon Strong thread
TAIL: Small bunch of deer hair
BODY: Mrs Simpson feathers, three groups of three feathers each side
HEAD & COLLAR: Natural deer hair, spun and clipped

This fly is great in dirty water around structure.

THE ENQUIRER

Tied by Adam Royter

HOOK: Mustad 94841NPBR, size 12
THREAD: Black or olive 6/0 Uni or Talon Strong thread
TAIL: Turkey breast feathers or brown partridge
BODY: Poly Glimmer or other flash tinsel material
OPPOSITIONAL WING: Marabou and Chickabou or Uni glow yarn and glow Sparkleflash
HEAD: Black deer hair

This fly rides on or just under the surface. Fish this fly in very shallow, flat water late in the afternoon and present the fly well ahead of the fish. Wait until the fish is within 2 m of the fly, then start a two finger figure-of-eight retrieve.

SIMPLE BLACK MUDDLER

Tied by Adam Royter

HOOK: Tiemco 9300, size 8–18
THREAD: Black
BODY: Black seal's fur, dubbed and picked out (optional)
HEAD & COLLAR: Texas whitetail deer hair, black

This is a quick and simple version capturing the essential elements of the original. For night fishing in lakes cast the fly as far as possible on a floating line. Retrieve figure-of-eight, as slowly as possible while keeping contact with the fly. In rivers on dark nights, fish in the smaller sizes, down and across backwaters and bubble lines.

CHAPTER 13

MUDEYES

BEC'S FAT SPIDER

HOOK: 8–10
THREAD: 6/0 red
BODY: Light green Furry Foam
LEGS: Pheasant tail fibres
THORAX: Dubbed green rabbit
EYES: Burnt mono—6 kg

A quick and easy to tie spider mudeye pattern that sinks slowly or can be greased to swim in the film. A slow figure-of-eight retrieve is best.

Tied by Adam Royter

CORDULIID

HOOK: Tiemco 9300, size 8–12
THREAD: Black
BODY: Hare's ear and brown seal's fur blend
LEGS: Deer hair
WING: Six black duck breast feathers
HEAD: Dubbing as body covered by three black duck breast feathers

This is a buoyant pattern that is fished slowly with short jerks along the surface at night. At dusk and dawn this fly can also work well when cast to rising fish.

Tied by David Dodd

HARE'S EAR MUDEYE

HOOK: Wet fly, size 8–10
THREAD: Black
BODY: Hare's ear fur
RIB: Fine copper wire
WING: Fur from base of hare's ear
HEAD: Hare's ear fur

Tied by Michael Milczuk

MATCHAM'S PEDDER MUDEYE FLOATING

HOOK: Mustad 80000, size 8
THREAD: Brown mono cord
BODY: Poly foam covered with brown Raffene, crocheted
LEGS: Deer hair
HEAD: Deer hair, spun and clipped

Tied by Laurie Matcham

Tied by David Dodd

MUDEYE AUSTRALIAN

HOOK: Size 8–10
THREAD: Black
TAIL: Rabbit fur
BODY: Rabbit fur
EYES: Adjustable plant ties
HEAD & THORAX: Dubbing rabbit and dark brown seal's fur

Tied by Peter Coulson

MUDEYE BITS

HOOK: Kamasan B175, size 8
THREAD: Black
BODY, LEGS & HEAD: All the leftover bits and pieces of your tying bench put into a dubbing loop and spun in a dubbing loop, wound on and picked out
EYES: Black plastic eyes

Tied by Peter Coulson

NZ MUDEYE

HOOK: Kamasan B175, size 8–12
THREAD: Red
TAIL: Black squirrel tail
BODY: Olive green and burgundy chenille, twisted
HACKLE: Black hen
HEAD: Red thread

This is one of my favourite mudeye patterns as it is very simple and catches lots of fish. The best retrieve is a medium speed figure-of-eight with the odd pause and fast strip.

Tied by Peter Coulson

PLAITED MUDEYE

HOOK: Tiemco, size 8–12
THREAD: Brown
BODY: Olive green and black chenille, plaited
THORAX: Rabbit fur dubbing, picked out
WING BUD: Pheasant breast feather
LEGS: Knotted pheasant tail
EYES: Black glass eyes wired on with copper wire

SLENDER MUDEYE

HOOK: Long shank 2X, size 8–12
THREAD: Black
TAIL: Two goose bolts, black
BODY: Rabbit fur, seal's fur and Antron mix spun in a dubbing loop, wound on and picked out
EYES: Black plastic eyes

Tied by Peter Coulson

SPIDER MUDEYE

HOOK: Kamasan B175, size 8–12
THREAD: Brown
BODY: HIVIS tied in a loop
THORAX & LEGS: Rabbit fur spun in a dubbing loop, wound on and picked out
EYES: Plastic eyes

Tied by Peter Coulson

STEINDL'S GREEN MUDEYE

HOOK: Wet, size 10–14
THREAD: Black
TAIL: Dyed green guinea fowl
BODY: Green chenille
BACK: Black chenille
HACKLE: Black duck breast feather

Tied by Michael Milczuk

WOVEN MUDEYE

HOOK: Tiemco, size 8–12
THREAD: Brown
BODY: Olive green and black chenille, woven
THORAX: Olive green rabbit dubbing, picked out
WING BUD: Pheasant breast feather
LEGS: Knotted pheasant tail
EYES: Brown glass eyes wired on with copper wire

Tied by Peter Coulson

CHAPTER 14

NIGHT FLIES

ANGEL

HOOK: Streamer, size 4–10
THREAD: Yellow monochord
TAIL: Black squirrel tail or hackle fibres
UNDERBODY: White cotton wool
BODY: Two coats of 'Polymark' Natural Glow No. PM501 (available from craft and haberdashery stores).
WING: Black squirrel tail
BEARD: Red or orange hackle fibres
HEAD: Coat with black fabric marker pen.

Charge the fly's body with a torch or camera flash—it is good for night fishing or discoloured water.

Tied by Andrew Lines

BLACK PHANTOM

HOOK: Size 2–8
THREAD: Black
TAIL: Black squirrel tail
UNDERBODY: Lead or copper wire (optional)
BODY: Black wool
RIB: Silver tinsel
WING: Two or three black feathers from the rump of a pukeko
CHEEKS: Jungle cock

Tied by David Dodd

CRAIG'S ALL BLACK

HOOK: Kamasan B175, size 6–10
THREAD: Black
UNDERBODY: Lead wire (optional)
BODY: Dubbed black seal's fur
WING: Three or four pukeko breast feathers

This fly is best fished after dark in the slow pools of rivers or lakes. The fly can be fished at all depths using a slow to very slow retrieve.

Tied by Lionel Coombs

CRAIG'S NIGHTTIME

HOOK: Tiemco 9300, size 6–10
THREAD: Black
TAIL: Red wool
UNDERBODY: Lead or copper wire (optional)
BODY: Black chenille or wool
RIB: Silver tinsel
WING: Three or four pukeko breast feathers
HACKLE: Black
TOPPING: Jungle cock eye, laid on top

Tied by David Dodd

CRAIG'S NIGHTTIME LUMO

Tied by Peter Coulson

HOOK: Kamasan B175, size 6–10
THREAD: Black
TAIL: Small tag of red wool
BODY: Lumo strip
WING: Three or four pukeko breast feathers

This fly is best fished after dark in the slow pools of rivers or lakes. It can be fished at all depths with all types of retrieves.

CRAZY ALIEN

Tied by Adam Royter

HOOK: Kamasan B830, size 8–12
THREAD: White 3/0
TAIL: Glow Flashabou, green
BODY: Jinkai Lumo beads, green
OVERWING: Glow Flashabou and pearl Aurora thread
HEAD: Holographic cement

This is the mother ship of the 'Glo' flies. This fly glows brightly and is good for fast retrieves or discoloured water. The Lumo beads are softer than the tube for those few extra seconds of chewing by the fish.

GLO FLY

Tied by Adam Royter

HOOK: Kamasan B830, size 4–6
THREAD: White 3/0
BODY: Jinkai Lumo tube, green
OVERWING: Green marabou
HEAD: Holographic cement

Solely a nighttime fly, this pattern has been responsible for dozens of fish of double figure weight. The Jinkai Lumo tube displays a long-lasting luminescence that other glow materials lack; it is also the most durable. Apart from the fly's individual ability to catch fish, in tandem rig formation this fly makes a good attractor for smaller, dark coloured flies to be fished on the point of your leader.

GLO FLY DELUX

Tied by Adam Royter

HOOK: Kamasan B830, size 4–6
THREAD: White 3/0
TAIL: Marabou purple
BODY: Jinkai Lumo tube, green
OVERWING: Marabou purple/black and silver holographic Flashabou
HEAD: Holographic cement

Same as the Glo Fly except this one looks more like a fly

GLOWING CADDIS

HOOK: Kamasan B400, size12
THREAD: Tan 6/0
RIDDING: Glow Flashabou, green
BODY: Antron, caddis green
WING: Glow Flashabou, green
HACKLE: White cock

Midsummer, when the caddis hatches are in full swing and the fish rise well into the night, is the perfect time to use the Glowing Caddis. I'm not too sure whether this fly is successful because the fish hit it more, or whether it is because I can see where it is going and have better fly placement. Either way, it works.

Tied by Adam Royter

GLOWING NIGHTTIME

HOOK: Gamakatsu F111, size 6
THREAD: Gudebrod 6/0, black
TAIL: Flashabou, glow in the dark orange
BODY: Crystal chenille pearl
OVERWING: Pukeko and jungle cock

This fly is one of the greatest nighttime flies of all time, it is an absolute winner.

Tied by Adam Royter

JULIAN BROWN'S DUNNY BRUSH

HOOK: Large dry fly hook, size 4–8
THREAD: Black
TAIL: Dark speckled turkey tail
BODY: Bronze peacock herl
WING: Dark speckled turkey tail, angled along body
HACKLE: Large black cock hackle

This fly is best for last light or after dark. Cast at sighted or audible rises in lakes or large pools. It can also be skated down and across in rivers at night.

Tied by Peter Coulson

LUMO GRUB

HOOK: Kamasan B175, size 8–12
THREAD: Black
BODY: Lumo strip
WING: Red marabou

Best fished after dark in rivers or lakes, this fly can be fished at all depths with all types of retrieves.

Tied by Matt Wales

Tied by Peter Coulson

PEACH NIGHT-TIME

HOOK: Kamasan B175, size 6–10
THREAD: Black
BODY: Peach chenille
RIB: Silver oval tinsel
WING: Three or four pukeko breast feathers

This fly is best fished during twilight and after dark in the slow pools of rivers or lakes. The retrieve should be slow to very slow on a floating line.

Tied by Peter Coulson

RED AND BLACK NIGHT FLY

HOOK: Wet fly, size 6–12
THREAD: Black
TAIL: Black possum
BODY HACKLE: Red cock, laid back
HEAD HACKLE: Black cock, laid back

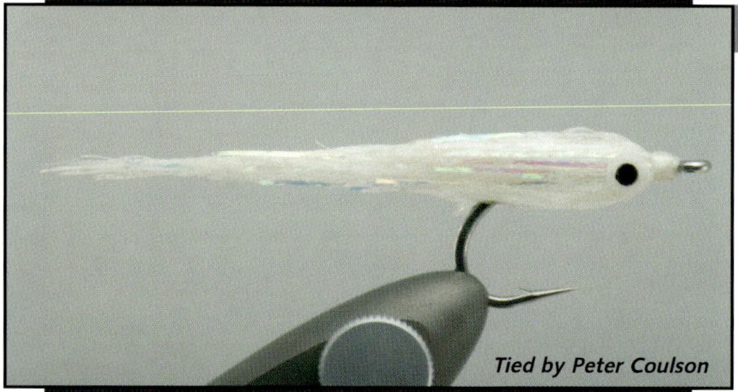

Tied by Peter Coulson

SKEETER GLOW

HOOK: Mustad C68S SS, size 6
THREAD: Flat, waxed white
BODY: Sparkleflash Glow in the Dark white pearl, tied shaggy dog style
EYES: Silver 2 mm, stick on
OVERBODY: Cover whole fly with two coats of SoftDip

Charge the body with a torch or camera flash. This fly sits in the surface film and leaves a small bow wave with each strip. Only strip this fly in short, 10 cm strips with a pause every fifth or sixth strip. Most strikes will happen on the pause. Because this fly is so buoyant it is great for the shallows after dark.

Tied by Adam Royter

STAR LIGHT

HOOK: Black Magic, size 6
THREAD: Uni-Thread 6/0, tan
TAIL: Flashabou, pearl
BODY: Killwell Lumo skirt
COLLAR: Rabbit fur, yellow and red

The Star Light uses one of the most luminescent fly tying materials in the world—the Killwell lumo skirt. This material was originally designed to be wrapped around a trolling lure and towed behind a boat, but I think it's much better wrapped around one of my flies.

BLACK NIGHT

HOOK: Kamasan B175, size 8–12
THREAD: Black
BODY: Black seal's fur
RIB: Silver oval tinsel
BODY HACKLE: Black cock
HEAD HACKLE: Black hen swept back

This is best fished after dark in small rivers with a slow retrieve.

Tied by Peter Coulson

HELMER

HOOK: Kamasan B175, size 6–10
THREAD: Black
TAIL: Small bunch of dark olive hackle fibres
BODY: Dark olive chenille
WING: Three peacock breast feathers tied in at the half way point and another three at the head

This fly can be fished at all depths with all types of retrieves, and is best fished after dark in the slow pools of rivers or lakes.

Tied by Peter Coulson

KIEWA GIANT

HOOK: Kamasan B175, size 10–16
THREAD: Black
BODY: Black seal's fur
WING & HEAD: Black fine deer hair

This is best fished in small rivers down and across at night.

Tied by Peter Coulson

NIGHT RAT

HOOK: Kamasan B175, size 6–10
THREAD: Black
TAIL: Small bunch of dark olive hackle fibres
BODY: Dark olive seal's fur dubbing
HACKLE: Dark olive hen spun in a dubbing loop and wound from tail to head

Tied by Peter Coulson

CHAPTER 15

NYMPHS

ANTRON BEAD HEAD NYMPH

HOOK: Kamasan B175, size 16–18
THREAD: Brown
TAIL: Brown hackle fibres
BODY: Fine copper Antron dubbing
RIB: Fine copper wire
THORAX: Fine copper Antron dubbing
HEAD: Small brass bead

BITZA

HOOK: TMC 5262, size 8–16
TAILS & LEGS: Round rubber
RIB: Copper wire
BODY & THORAX: Black possum
WINGCASE: Pearl Krystal Flash
HEAD: Gold bead

BLACK NYMPH (DODD)

HOOK: Tiemco 2302, size 12–14
THREAD: Black
TAIL: Black cock hackle fibre
BODY: Black rabbit
RIB: Fine copper wire
THROAT HACKLE: Black hen
WINGCASE: Crow feather
HEAD: Black tying thread
TYING NOTE: May be weighted with copper or lead wire

BEAD BOMB

HOOK: Tiemco 2302, size 10–12
THREAD: Black
TAIL: Red hives
BUTT: Black dubbing
BODY: Three black glass beads
HEAD: Medium size brass bead

Tied by Peter Coulson

BLACK BOMB

HOOK: Kamasan B175, size 10–12
THREAD: Black
TAIL: Black cock fibres
BODY: Copper wire coated in black nail polish

This fly is great for getting down quickly. It is best fished with a small unweighted nymph trailing behind.

Tied by Ty Smith

BOMB 1

HOOK: Curved nymph hook, size 10
HEAD: Medium brass bead
THREAD: Uni-Thread 6/0
TAIL: Moose body hair
ABDOMEN: Chestnut Antron and epoxy on top
LEGS: Moose body hair
WINGCASE: Moose body hair and epoxy
RIB: Fine gold wire
THORAX: Chestnut Antron
WEIGHT: Heavy lead wire

Tied by Ty Smith

BOMB2

HOOK: Curved nymph hook, size 10
HEAD: Medium black bead
THREAD: Uni-thread 6/0
TAIL: Moose body hair
ABDOMEN: Hare's ear
LEGS: Moose body hair
WINGCASE: Moose body hair and epoxy
RIB: Copper wire
THORAX: Hare's ear
WEIGHT: Heavy lead wire

Tied by Ty Smith

BOMB 3

HOOK: Curved nymph hook, size 10
HEAD: Medium copper bead
THREAD: Uni-thread 6/0
TAIL: Pheasant tail, dyed green
ABDOMEN: Olive seal's fur
LEGS: Pheasant tail, dyed green
WINGCASE: Pheasant tail dyed green and epoxy
RIB: Copper wire
THORAX: Olive seal's fur
WEIGHT: Heavy lead wire

BRASS NYMPH

HOOK: Tiemco B175, size 12–16
THREAD: Dark red
BUTT: Red thread
BODY: Five brass beads
HEAD: Red thread

This fly works very well in fast water and is very easy to tie.

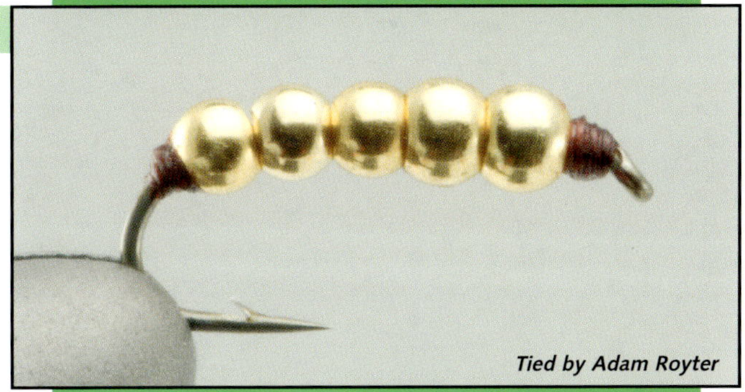

Tied by Adam Royter

BROWN AND COPPER

HOOK: Kamasan B175, size 12–16
THREAD: Black
TAIL: Brown hackle fibres
UNDERBODY: Copper wire (optional)
BODY: Dubbed brown seal's fur
RIB: Fine copper wire
THORAX: Peacock herl
HACKLE: Brown cock hackle
HEAD: Black thread

This fly works very well on stillwater around weedbeds.

Tied by Peter Coulson

CASUAL DRESS NYMPH (RUMPF)

HOOK: Kamasan B820, size 12, slightly bent upwards in the middle
THREAD: Black
TAIL: Pine squirrel
BODY: Dubbed pine squirrel
COLLAR: Pine squirrel
HEAD: Black ostrich herl, clipped
EYES: Luminous Twinkle by Lureflash

Tied by Peter Coulson

CLARET & TUNGSTEN BEAD HEAD NYMPH

HOOK: Kamasan B175, size 10
THREAD: Brown Uni-Thread 6/0
TAIL: Mallard duck breast feathers
BODY: Brown possum dubbing
RIB: Dull copper wire
THORAX: Claret dubbing
HEAD: Gold 3 mm tungsten bead

Tied by Neil Grose

Tied by Peter Coulson

COPPER BEAD HARE'S EAR

HOOK: Kamasan B175, size 16–20
THREAD: Black
TAIL: Partridge breast feather fibres
BODY: Hare's ear dubbing, picked out
RIB: Fine copper wire
HEAD: Small, 2 mm copper bead

This fly is best fished in small clear alpine streams down and across.

Tied by Peter Coulson

COPPER BOMB

HOOK: Kamasan B830, size 10–14
THREAD: Black
TAIL: Ringneck pheasant tail barbs
BODY: Copper wire
THORAX: Hare's ear dubbing, copper bead, hare's ear dubbing
HACKLE: Partridge breast feather

This fly is best fished in rivers down and across or up stream in fast water. This fly gets down very quickly.

Tied by Andrew Lines

COPPERHEAD NYMPH

HOOK: Long shank, size 10–12
THREAD: Black Monocord
TAIL: Four deer hairs splayed
BODY: Two black ostrich herls
RIB: Medium copper wire
THORAX & HEAD: Medium copper wire

This fly is best fished under a strike indicator or dry fly in rivers and lakes. It can be fished on a sinking line using medium speed strips.

Tied by Neil Grose

DEEP WATER NYMPH

HOOK: Tiemco 200R, size 10–12
THREAD: Brown Uni-Thread 6/0
TAIL: Straight brown possum fur
UNDERBODY: Copper wire
BODY: Dark brown possum fur
RIB: Dull copper wire
THORAX: Claret seal's fur
WINGCASE: Pearl Flashback

DRIFTER 2

HOOK: Curved nymph hook, size 12–14
HEAD: Small brass or copper bead
THREAD: Uni-Thread 6/0
TAIL: Pheasant tail
ABDOMEN: Pheasant tail
LEGS: Pheasant tail
WINGCASE: Pheasant tail and epoxy
RIB: Copper wire
THORAX: Peacock herl
WEIGHT: Medium lead wire

Tied by Ty Smith

DRIFTER 3

HOOK: Curved nymph hook, size 12–14
HEAD: Small brass or copper bead
THREAD: Uni-Thread 6/0
TAIL: Pheasant tail dyed green
ABDOMEN: Pheasant tail
LEGS: Pheasant tail dyed green
WINGCASE: Pheasant tail dyed green and epoxy
RIB: Copper wire
THORAX: Peacock herl
WEIGHT: Medium lead wire

Tied by Ty Smith

DRIFTER 4

HOOK: Curved nymph hook, size 12–14
HEAD: Small brass or copper bead
THREAD: Uni-Thread 6/0
TAIL: Dark brown pheasant tail
ABDOMEN: Fiery brown seal's fur
LEGS: Dark brown pheasant tail
WINGCASE: Pearl Flash, over brown pheasant tail and epoxy
SHELL BACK: Pearl Flash
RIB: Copper wire
THORAX: Fiery brown seal's fur
WEIGHT: Medium lead wire

Tied by Ty Smith

FLEXI FLOSS NYMPH

HOOK: Tiemco, size 10–12
THREAD: Black
TAIL: Ginger cock fibres
BODY: Light brown seal's fur
RIB: Gold Flexi Floss
WINGCASE: Gold Flexi Floss
HEAD: Black

Tied by Peter Coulson

Tied by Daryl Grant

GLASS HEAD NYMPH

HOOK: Kamasan B175, size 10–14
THREAD: Black
TAIL: Brown hackle fibre
BODY: Brown rabbit dubbing
RIB: Gold wire
HEAD: Dark glass bead

This fly is best fished in small highland rivers down and across in slow to medium water.

Tied by Michael Milczuk

GOLD RIBBED HARE'S EAR

HOOK: Wet, size 12–18
THREAD: Cahill 8/0
BODY: Fur from the base of a hare's ear
RIB: Gold tinsel
THORAX: As for body
HACKLE: Guard hairs, picked out

Tied by David Dodd

GOLD HEAD PHEASANT TAIL

HOOK: Tiemco 9300, size 12–14
THREAD: Black
TAIL: Pheasant tail
BODY: Pheasant tail
RIB: Fine copper wire
THORAX: Krystal Dub fiery brown
HEAD: Medium gold bead

This is a good fly for deep nymphing.

Tied by Peter Coulson

GREEN POSSUM NYMPH

HOOK: Kamasan B175, size 10–12
THREAD: Black
TAIL: Natural possum
BODY: Natural possum and olive seal's fur blend
WING CASE: Natural possum
HEAD: Black

GREEN SURFACE NYMPH

HOOK: Partridge nymph 12
THREAD: Olive 6/0
TAIL: Squirrel Blend dubbing, olive
PALMER: Olive C.D.C.
UNDERBODY: Squirrel Blend dubbing, olive

This fly was designed to attract fast moving, surface feeding trout by making a distinct 'V' line in the water when stripped fast and full.

Tied by Adam Royter

HAIRY DOG

HOOK: Nymph size 12–14
THREAD: Black 6/0
TAIL: Pheasant tail fibres, natural
RIB: Fine copper wire
DUBBING: Mix equal amounts of hare's ear colour Antron and the fur from a hare's mask
WINGCASE: Pheasant tail

A good all-rounder nondescript nymph, the Hairy Dog works fished down deep or in the surface film.

Tied by Adam Royter

HARE & COPPER BEAD HEAD

HOOK: Tiemco 9300, size 12–16
THREAD: Black or brown
TAIL: Red cock hackle fibre
BODY: Hare's ear dubbing
RIB: Copper wire
THORAX: Hare's ear dubbing, picked out
HEAD: Medium copper bead

This is a good fly for deep nymphing.

Tied by David Dodd

HARE'S EAR NYMPH

HOOK: Tiemco 5262, size 12–16
THREAD: Black or brown
TAIL: Red cock hackle fibre
BODY: Hare's ear dubbing
RIB: Gold tinsel
THORAX: Hare's ear dubbing picked out
WINGCASE: Brown feather fibre
HEAD: Black tying thread
TYING NOTE: May be weighted with copper or lead wire

Tied by David Dodd

HARE'S EAR (GOLD BEAD HEAD)

HOOK: Tiemco 5262, size 12–16
THREAD: Black or brown
TAIL: Red cock hackle fibre
BODY: Hare's ear dubbing
RIB: Gold tinsel
THORAX: Hare's ear dubbing, picked out
HEAD: Medium gold bead

Good fly for deep nymphing

Tied by David Dodd

JETSON EMERGER NYMPH

HOOK: Dry fly, size 10–16
THREAD: Black 8/0
TAIL: Black squirrel tail
BODY: Tan possum dubbing
RIB: Fine copper wire
THROAT: Light brown possum dub
WING: Brown HIVIS

Tied by Noel Jetson

KB NYMPH

HOOK: Long shank, size 14–16
THREAD: Brown 8/0
TAIL: Brown cock fibres
BODY: Single ply of brown knitting wool
RIB: Fine copper wire
THORAX: Peacock herl over 0.20 mm lead wire
HEAD: Gold bead 3–3.5 mm

This fly was designed to fish fast water. Fish it upstream below an indicator.

Tied by Ian Mitchell

LITTLE BLACK DRESS

HOOK: Long shank, size 14
THREAD: Black 8/0
TAIL: Black hen fibres
UNDERBODY: Fine lead wire, 6–7 turns
BODY: Single ply of black knitting wool or black floss
RIB: Fine copper wire
THORAX: Black seal's fur
WINGCASE: Holographic tinsel, 2 strands
HACKLE: Black hen
HEAD: Black thread varnished

This a great fly for small streams in Victoria's south east.

Tied by Ian Mitchell

MINI BEAD HEAD NYMPH BLACK

HOOK: Kamasan B175, size 16–18
THREAD: Black
TAIL: Black hackle fibres
BODY: Fine black dubbing
RIB: Fine gold tinsel
THORAX: Fine black dubbing
HEAD: Small brass bead

This fly works on the principle that elephants eat peanuts.

Tied by Peter Coulson

MINI BEAD HEAD NYMPH BROWN

HOOK: Kamasan B175, size 16–18
THREAD: Black
TAIL: Brown hackle fibres
BODY: Fine brown dubbing
RIB: Fine copper wire
THORAX: Fine brown dubbing
HEAD: Small brass bead

This fly works on the principle that elephants eat peanuts.

Tied by Peter Coulson

MINK NYMPH

HOOK: Tiemco 2302, size 12–14
THREAD: Black or brown
TAIL: Dark dun cock hackle fibre
BODY: Mink dark brown
RIB: Fine copper wire
THROAT HACKLE: Partridge
WINGCASE: Brown turkey or hen pheasant fibre
HEAD: Black tying thread
TYING NOTE: May be weighted with copper or lead wire

Tied by David Dodd

OLIVE NYMPH

HOOK: Tiemco 2302, size 12–14
THREAD: Black
TAIL: Olive cock hackle fibre
BODY: Olive rabbit
RIB: Fine copper wire
THROAT HACKLE: Olive hen or partridge
WINGCASE: Swan dyed olive with Dylon 34
HEAD: Black tying thread
TYING NOTE: May be weighted with copper or lead wire

Tied by David Dodd

Tied by Peter Coulson

PARTRIDGE BEAD HEAD NYMPH

HOOK: Kamasan B175, size 10–14
THREAD: Black
TAIL: Partridge
BODY: Natural rabbit
RIB: Fine copper wire
THROAT HACKLE: Partridge
HEAD: Brass bead

This fly is best fished upstream, nymphing style, in medium to large river

Tied by Michael Milczuk

PHEASANT TAIL NYMPH

HOOK: Wet fly, size 12–16
THREAD: Black
TAIL: Pheasant tail fibres
BODY: Build up shape with red transformer wire
WINGCASE: Wrap over with the pheasant tail fibres

Tied by Peter Coulson

PHEASANT TAIL NYMPH GREEN

HOOK: Wet fly, size 14–16
THREAD: Black
TAIL: Pheasant tail fibres dyed green
RIB: Green wire
BODY: Build up shape with red transformer wire, ther wrap over with the dyed green pheasant tail fibres

Tied by David Dodd

PHEASANT TAIL VARIANT

HOOK: Tiemco 9300, size 12–16
THREAD: Black
TAIL: Pheasant tail
BODY: Pheasant tail
RIB: Fine copper wire
THORAX: Krystal Dub, fiery brown
WINGCASE: Pheasant tail
LEGS: Fibre from wing case tied back after wing case has been formed
HEAD: Black thread

PHILBRICK'S NYMPH

HOOK: Wet fly, size 10–16
THREAD: Black
TAIL: 6–8 brown cock fibres
BODY: Blend red, brown, green and black seal's fur. Keep body thin
THORAX: Blend red, brown, green and black seal's fur. Keep body thin

This fly was designed to be fished inert for tailing fish in the central plateau of Tasmania.

Tied by John Philbrick

POWDERBEAD NYMPH

HOOK: Tiemco 2302, size 12
THREAD: Black
TAIL: Light cock hackle fibre
BODY: Three small, yellow, powder coated brass beads
THORAX: Natural rabbit under two powder coated brass beads, with the rabbit teased out
WINGCASE: Duck breast feathers
HEAD: Black

Tied by Adam Royter

POWDERHEAD NYMPH GOLD

HOOK: Tiemco 2302, size 12
THREAD: Black
TAIL: Pheasant tail
BODY: Gold Antron blend teased out
RIB: Copper wire
WINGCASE: Crow
HEAD: Gold powder coated brass bead

Tied by Adam Royter

POWDERHEAD NYMPH GREEN

HOOK: Tiemco 2302, size 12
THREAD: Black
TAIL: Light green cock hackle fibre
BODY: Green Antron blend, teased out
RIB: Pearl tinsel
WINGCASE: Crow
HEAD: Olive powder coated brass bead

Tied by Adam Royter

POWDERHEAD NYMPH GREY

Tied by Adam Royter

HOOK: Tiemco 2302, size 12
THREAD: Black
TAIL: Light grey cock hackle fibre
BODY: Grey Antron blend teased out
RIB: Gold tinsel
WINGCASE: Crow
HEAD: Olive powder coated brass bead

RABBIT AND SEAL

Tied by Peter Coulson

HOOK: Kamasan B400, size 12–16
THREAD: Black
BODY: Red and black seal's fur dubbing, picked out
RIB: Pearl Lure flash
HEAD: Rabbit fur, dubbed

This fly is a good all-round lake fly, best fished very slowly.

REDHEAD NYMPH

Tied by Adam Royter

HOOK: Tiemco 2302, size 10–12
THREAD: Black
TAIL: Black cock fibres
BUTT: Black dubbing
BODY: Three glass beads black, blue, black, with black Antron dubbing between each bead and teased out.
HEAD: Medium size brass bead coloured red with nail polish

RIPPLE NYMPH

Tied by Gerd Behnecke

HOOK: Kamasan B 175, size 10–14
THREAD: Black
TAIL: Fiery brown cock hackle fibres
BODY: Fiery brown seal's fur
WING CASE: Black crow feather
RIB: Flat copper tinsel
BEARD: Fiery brown cock hackle fibres

Best fished slowly in and around weed beds in lakes on a floating line. This fly will swim upside down due to the beard hackle and helps avoid snags.

RUBBER LEG NYMPH

HOOK: Tiemco, size 10–12
THREAD: Black
TAIL: Red cock
BODY: Red and black dubbing mix
LEGS: Fine black rubber
WINGCASE: Black raffia
HEAD: Black

Best fished at dead drift in rivers. The rubber legs supply all the movement.

Tied by Peter Coulson

SPARKLE NYMPH

HOOK: Tiemco, size 10–12
THREAD: Olive green
BODY: Lime green and bright green Antron mix
LEGS: Knotted pheasant tail
THORAX: Natural rabbit
WINGCASE: Turkey wing feather doubled over
EYES: Black mono eyes
HEAD: Olive green

Tied by Adam Royter

SWIMMER NYMPH

HOOK: Daiichi 1770, size 12–18
THREAD: Black or brown
TAIL: Red cock hackle fibres
BODY: Brown nymph dubbing, teased out at the thorax
RIB: Fine copper wire
WEIGHT: Lead wire (optional)
WINGCASE: Mottled brown turkey tail

Tied by Ezra Bibby

SWIMMING NYMPH

HOOK: Daiichi 1750, size 10–12
THREAD: Black
TAIL: Fiery Brown cock hackle fibres
BODY: Brown rabbit
THORAX: Brown rabbit
WINGCASE: Pheasant
THROAT HACKLE: Fiery brown cock hackle fibres

Best fished in lakes on a floating line with a slow retrieve.

Tied by Daryl Grant

CHAPTER 16

SCUD, GRUB, SHRIMP, YABBIES, TADPOLES

ANDY SHRIMP

HOOK: Gamakatsu, size 12–14
THREAD: Black 6/0
LEGS: Light tan cock hackle
RIB: Silver flat tinsel
BODY: Devcon epoxy

Tied by Peter Coulson

ANTRON SCUD

HOOK: Scud, size 12–14
THREAD: Black 6/0
BODY & LEGS: Light olive and brown Anton dubbing, teased out for legs
RIB: Midge lace
HEAD: Black 6/0 thread

Tied by Michael Milczuk

APPOSING SCUD

HOOK: Grub, size 12–16
THREAD: Tan 6/0
BODY: Hare's mask dubbed and teased out for legs
RIB: 1 kg mono
BACK: Cling Wrap
FEELERS: Hare guard hairs

This is best cast in front of tailing fish and retrieved slowly with a figure-of-eight action.

Tied by Peter Coulson

BACKSWIMMER

HOOK: Wet, size 12–16
THREAD: Orange 6/0
BODY: Light olive dubbing
RIB: Silver tinsel
BELLY: White poly yarn
HEAD: Black 6/0 thread

Tied by Michael Milczuk

Tied by Adam Royter

CLING WRAP SHRIMP

HOOK: Long shank, size 2–8
THREAD: 1 kg nylon fishing line
FEELERS: Pearl Aurora thread
FRONT LEGS: Bucktail fibres
EYES: Burnt mono, 10 kg
LEGS: White Polar Fibre or Mara Wool
SHELL & BODY: Cling Wrap

Fishing this fly deep along weedbeds in lakes. Best strip technique is a 30 cm fast strip followed by a sit for 3–4 seconds.

Tied by Michael Milczuk

CLIVE'S RAINBOW SHRIMP

HOOK: Wet extra long, size 8–12
THREAD: Black 6/0
TAIL: Turkey tail quill slip
BODY: Seal's fur, light brown, yellow and green
RIB: Fine gold wire
FEELERS: Pheasant tail fibres

Tied by Andrew Lines

CO-POLYMER SHRIMP

HOOK: Caddis grub hook, size 12
THREAD: Black mono cord
BODY HACKLE: Palmered Cree cock clipped on the top and sides
RIB: Oval silver tinsel
BACK: Selleys co-polymer sealant
TYING NOTE: Run a bead of co-polymer sealant along the top and sides then allow this to skin. Gently push it into shape with your finger. The co-polymer takes a couple of days to dry.

Best fished with a short jerky motion on a floating line. This fly is meant to swim upside down to avoid snagging.

Tied by Michael Milczuk

DUCKMALOI TADPOLE

HOOK: Kamasan B175, size 12–16
THREAD: Black 6/0
TAIL: Four or five black marabou herl threads
BODY: Black marabou herl wrapped and palmered with a dark dun cock hackle
FRONT HACKLE: White hen, two turns only

GIBSON'S BACKSWIMMER

HOOK: Kamasan B175, size 12–18
THREAD: White 8/0
BODY: White dubbing
RIB: Pearl tinsel
LEGS: Pheasant tail fibres
BACK: Black crow wing fibres

Tied by Bruce Gibson

GREEN MEANIE

HOOK: Down eye wet, size 2–12
THREAD: Dark green
TAIL: Red cock hackle fibres
LEGS: Red cock hackle fibres
BODY: Fine dark green chenille
RIB: 28lb Platil Strong mono
EYES: Powder-coated yellow or chartreuse dumbbell eyes

Tied to imitate either a small shrimp or a nymph, it is best fished around weed beds, either dead drift or a slow, twitchy retrieve. Use the smaller sizes for trout and up to size 2 for estuary species.

Tied by Chris Ellemor

GREEN SCUD

HOOK: Scud hook, size 12
THREAD: Olive green
RIB: 1 kg nylon fishing line
BODY: Olive green dubbing
FRONT LEGS: Dubbing picked out
LEGS: Dubbing picked out
BACK: Olive green raffia

Tied by Adam Royter

HARE'S EAR SCUD

HOOK: Kamasan B175, size 12–18
THREAD: Black 8/0
BODY: Hare's ear dubbing
RIB: Fine gold wire
LEGS: Hare's ear
BACK: Hare's ear

Tied by Peter Coulson

Tied by Adam Royter

HOVER

HOOK: Kamasan B175, size 10–14
THREAD: 1 kg nylon fishing line
FEELERS: Pearl tinsel
FRONT LEGS: Olive green rabbit
EYES: Mono eyes
LEGS: Olive green rabbit
SHELL & BODY: E-Z Body and coated in Softex

This pattern catches air in the body which makes the fly hover. Great for fishing over weedbeds.

Tied by Noel Jetson

JETSON NYMBEET

HOOK: Nymph hook, size 10–14
THREAD: Black 8/0
TAIL: Black cock hackle fibres
BODY: Thin strip of clear plastic, wrapped
HACKLE: Black cock, throat style
BACK: Black crow wing fibres

Tied by J M Gillies

J M GILLIES SCUD

HOOK: Partridge limerick, size 10–12
THREAD: Black
TAIL: Dyed olive cock hackle fibres
BODY: Multi-mix of wool dubbing
LEGS: Clipped dyed olive cock hackle feather tied under from tail to head
HEAD: Black thread

Tied by Adam Royter

LARGE GREEN SHRIMP

HOOK: Long shank, size 2-8
THREAD: Black
FEELERS: Mix of olive and brown marabou with green Antron fibres
BODY: Olive green dubbing mix
EYES: Red glass beads on burnt mono
RIB: Green wire
SHELL & BACK: Green glass beads covered with thin plastic sheet cut to shape
LEGS: Olive green marabou

This pattern fishes best in dirty water.

MARA SHRIMP

HOOK: Mustad, size 2–8
THREAD: Black
BODY: Olive green chenille
RIB: Copper wire
FEELERS: Olive green marabou
BACK: Pearl Krystal Flash
HACKLE: Olive green grizzle

Tied by Peter Coulson

MONO SHRIMP

HOOK: Long shank, size 10–12
THREAD: 1 kg nylon fishing line
FEELERS: Pearl Krystal Flash and Mara wool
REAR LEGS: Mara wool
EYES: Burnt mono, 10 kg
SHELL & BODY: 1 kg mono coloured red in the middle

Best strip technique is a 30 cm fast strip and before sitting for 3–4 seconds.

Tied by Adam Royter

NYMBEET

HOOK: Kamasan B175, size 10–14
THREAD: Black 3/0
TAIL: Six black cock fibres
BACK: A strip of black crow doubled over length-ways
BODY: Clear midge lace
HACKLE: Black cock, two turns and clipped on top

Tied by Peter Coulson

NEW ENGLAND YABBY

HOOK: Wet extra long, size 12–8
THREAD: Black 6/0
TAIL: Squirrel tail, tied on in two bunches, one each side
BODY: Grey possum fur
HACKLE: Three separate wrappings of badger hackle, each swept well back separated by dubbing
EYES: Brass bead chain

Tied by Michael milczuk

POLAR FIBRE SHRIMP

HOOK: Long shank, size 8–12
THREAD: Olive
BODY & FEELERS: Olive green Polar Fibre over tan Polar Fibre
RIB: 1 kg nylon fishing line
EYES: Burnt mono, 10 kg

POLARPLUS SHRIMP

HOOK: Wet long shank, size 2–8
THREAD: Tan 6/0
FEELERS: Pearl Aurora thread
EYES: Burnt mono 20kg
LEGS: Polar Fibre, brown
BODY: Polar Fibre, brown dubbing
RIBBING: Uni-Flex red
SHELL: Polar Fibre, olive

Originally designed for estuary use, this small prawn does a good job of imitating a trout sized yabby and has proved successful in many lakes.

ROB'S GRUB

HOOK: Caddis grub hook, size 10–14
THREAD: Yellow mono cord
UNDERBODY: Lead or copper wire
BODY: White reflective tape. Available from automotive and safety equipment suppliers. Lightly coat body with fluorescent yellow or green nail polish.
BEARD: Partridge or wood duck breast feather
HEAD: Black fabric pen

This fly is good for clear, stony streams. I generally fish this pattern in riffles near the bottom.

SCARY SHRIMP

HOOK: Nymph, size 10–14
THREAD: 1 kg nylon fishing line
EYES: Burnt mono 4 kg
FEELERS: Bucktail fibres
MIDDLE BANDING: Red Flashabou
LEGS & SWIMMERS: White Polar Fibre or Mara Wool
BODY: Cling Wrap
SHELL: Five minute epoxy

This fly is a good pattern to fish in shallow water when fish are chasing shrimp and is best fished in very short fast strips.

SCUD (AMPHIPOD)

HOOK: Short shank dry, size 12–16
THREAD: Clear mono 1lb
BODY: Clear mouthguard material (EVA)
WING: Black over orange Slinky Fibre
EYES: Black waterproof marker (optional)
BODY COLOUR: Clear, red or olive Antron dubbed on the hook shank (optional)

Fish with either sinking or floating line, extremely slowly. Watch the end of your line at all times.

Tied by Graeme Clifford

SCUDRAPOD

HOOK: Nymph hook 12–16
THREAD: Black 8/0
BODY: Olive ostrich herl wrapped
RIB: Black thread
BACK: Two coats of Soft Tex

Tied by Muz Wilson

THE SCUD

HOOK: Gamakatsu, size 10–16
THREAD: White
FEELERS: Olive green hackle fibres
BODY: Light coloured dubbing
BACK: Clear Scud Back
RIB: Fine copper wire
EYES: Burnt mono 10 kg
LEGS: Dubbing picked out

Tied by Peter Coulson

CHAPTER 17

SMELT

ANDY'S RABBIT

HOOK: Long down eye, size 6–10
THREAD: Yellow or pearl metallised polyester sewing thread
TAIL: Six strands of pearl Krystal Flash
BODY: Same as thread
WING: Olive green or grey rabbit fur tied in clumps along shank
EYES: Yellow and black fabric paint pen
HEAD: Black fabric paint pen

This fly is best fished down and across adding action with rod tip.

Tied by Andrew Lines

BLACK NOSE DACE

HOOK: Streamer hook, size 8
THREAD: Black
TAIL: Red wool, short
BODY: Flat silver tinsel
WING: Black bucktail over white bucktail

Use this fly on a sinking leader. When you see a fish move, or disturbed baitfish, cast in the general direction and allow the fly to sink. Retrieve with short, sharp strips.

Tied by Alistair Purvey

BMS GREY

HOOK: TMC 5262, size 8
TAIL & BODY: BMS blend or SLF
RIB: Gold or silver Mylar
THROAT: Red silk
HEAD: Glass bead, clear

Tied By Muz Wilson

BMS OLIVE

HOOK: TMC 5262, size 8
TAIL & BODY: BMS blend or SLF
RIB: Gold or silver Mylar
THROAT: Red silk
HEAD: Glass bead, clear

Tied By Muz Wilson

BMS WHITE

HOOK: TMC 5262, size 8
TAIL & BODY: BMS blend or SLF
RIB: Gold or silver Mylar
THROAT: Red silk
HEAD: Glass bead, clear

CALFTAIL SMELT

HOOK: Partridge, size 10–14
THREAD: Black
BUTT: Two turns of oval silver tinsel
TAIL: Grey cock fibres
BODY: White floss
RIB: Oval silver tinsel
WING: White calf tail
THROAT: Grey cock fibres
HEAD: Black thread

This fly is best fished down and across in rivers.

GRANT SMELT

HOOK: Kamasan B830, size 12
THREAD: Black
TAIL: Red rabbit
BODY: Gold tinsel
WING: White SLF
THROAT: Yellow rabbit
HEAD: Black

This fly works well in dirty water early in the season. The best fishing method is down and across in medium to slow water with a figure-of-eight retrieve.

GREAT WESTERN SMELT

HOOK: Gamakatsu F111, size 6–10
THREAD: Uni 6/0 tan
UNDERBODY: Poly Glimmer peacock
TAIL & BODY: Polar Fibre white, olive and shrimp
TAIL FLASH: Flashabou holographic silver
THROAT: Comes Alive, red
EYES: 3D silver

This is an imitation of the large, most popular minnow, the common Galaxias. The best retrieve is a medium to fast strip.

MERRI MINNOW

HOOK: TMC 700B, size 8
BODY: Pearl Accent Flash
WING: Chinchilla rabbit Zonka
OVERWING: Olive kangaroo
THROAT: Red ostrich
HEAD: Olive dubbing

Tied by Muz Wilson

MICK'S COMMON GALAXIAS (YELLOW)

HOOK: Tiemco TMC #9349 4X long, size 10–6
TAIL: A few strands of yellow Crystal hair
BODY: Yellow Crystal Hair with Devcon epoxy over
UNDERWING 1: Yellow Fish Fuzz fibres tied over to just past the tail
UNDERWING 2: Olive HIVIS fibres tied over and just past the first underwing
OVERWING: Olive Fish Hair fibres tied to just short of the end of the underwings
EYES: Size 2 silver black stick on eyes
HEAD: Devcon epoxy over eyes and head to hold the wing fibres close to the body.

Tied by Mick Hall

MARDI GRAS MINNOW

HOOK: Black Magic B, size 8–2
THREAD: 3/0 White
TAIL: Chartreuse marabou and pearl Aurora thread
BODY: Pearl Mylar tubing and dubbed red marabou
OVER WING: Wood duck chest feathers
THROAT HACKLE: Pink and black hackle fibres

This fly was developed about the time when Rapala released their FT (fire tiger) colour. The lure proved very effective on both lake and stream. Lots of similar fly patterns were devised in the following months; this was the first fly pattern to do well.

Tied by Adam Royter

MICK'S DARK SMELT

HOOK: Tiemco TMC #9349 4X long, size 10–6
TAIL: A few strands of ice blue Crystal Hair
BODY: Pearl Crystal Hair coated with Devcon epoxy
UNDERWING 1: Pale olive Crystal Hair tied over back to just past the tail
UNDERWING 2: Olive HIVIS fibres tied over and a fraction longer than the first underwing
OVERWING: Brown Fish Hair fibres tied to just short of the underwings
EYES: Size 2 silver black stick on eyes
HEAD: Devcon epoxy over eyes and head and slightly over the back of the wings to hold the wing fibres close to the body.

Tied by Mick Hall

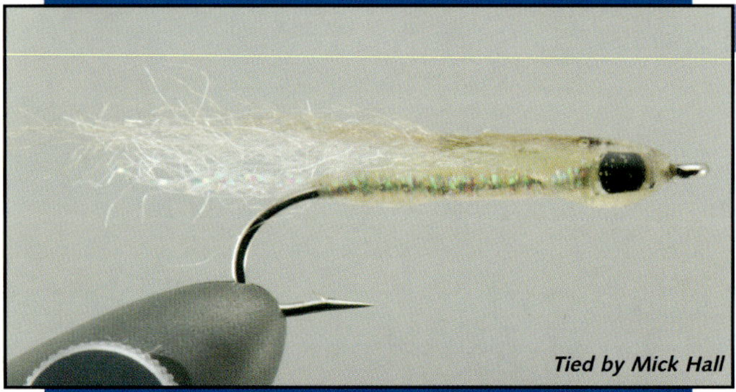

Tied by Mick Hall

MICK'S GLASSY SMELT

HOOK: Tiemco TMC #9349 Straight eye nickel plated 4X long, size 10 or smaller.
TAIL: Few strands of pearl Crystal Hair
BODY: Strands of pearl Crystal Hair with a thin layer of Devcon epoxy
UNDERWING: Fluorescent white HIVIS fibres tied over body to just past end of tail
OVERWING: Dark dun HIVIS fibres tied over to just past the underwing
EYES: Size 2 silver black, stick on eyes, trim to make eyes smaller
HEAD: Devcon epoxy over eyes and head to hold the wing fibres close to the body

Tied by Mick Hall

MICK'S PALE SMELT

HOOK: Tiemco TMC #9349 straight eye nickel plated 4X long, size 10–6
TAIL: A few strands of ice blue Crystal Hair
BODY: White silk with a thin layer of Devcon epoxy
UNDERWING: Pale olive Crystal Hair tied over back to just past tail
OVERWING: Olive HIVIS fibres tied over to just past the underwing
EYES: Size 2 silver black stick on eyes, trim to make eyes smaller
HEAD: Devcon epoxy over eyes and head and slightly over the back of the wings to hold the wing fibres close to the body

Tied by Adam Royter

MILLENNIUM MINNOW

HOOK: 2X long, size 6
THREAD: 6/0 white
TAIL: Red marabou
BODY: Flashabou holographic silver
OVERBODY: Chartreuse rabbit fur (Zonker strip) and lime Flashabou dubbing
UNDERBODY: White S.L.F
SIDE HACKLE: Grizzle cock
EYES: 3D silver

This fly works as an attractor pattern that draws the fish's attention away from the school of fish it is chasing, to come and eat it instead. Sounds crazy, but it works.

Tied by Peter Coulson

PETE'S SMELT

HOOK: Kamasan B175, size 8–10
THREAD: Blood red
TAIL: Two grey cock feathers
BODY: Silver SLF dubbing
RIB: Silver oval tinsel
HEAD: Blood red thread

This fly is best fished in winter with a short sharp retrieve followed by a long pause.

SKEETER GREY BACK

HOOK: Mustad C68S SS, size 6
THREAD: White flat waxed
BODY: Sparkleflash bellyshine, tied shaggy dog style
EYES: Silver 2 mm stick on
COLOUR: 70% grey waterproof marker on the back before you apply SoftDip
OVERBODY: Cover whole fly with 2 coats of SoftDip

This fly sits in the surface film and leaves a small bow wave with each strip. Only strip this fly in short, 10 cm strips pausing every fifth or sixth strip. Most strikes will occur on the pause. Because this fly is so buoyant it is great for the shallows.

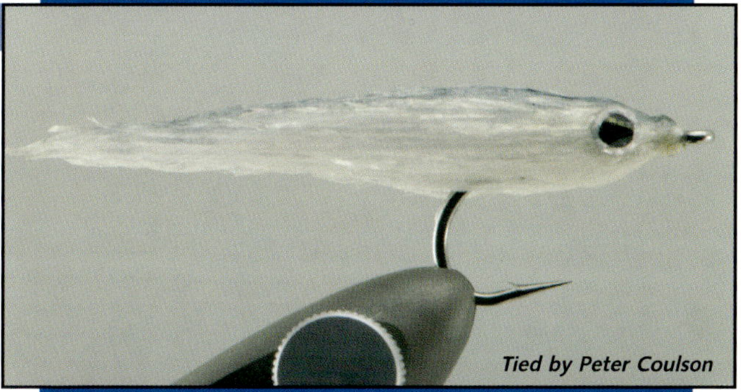

Tied by Peter Coulson

THE SNOW SMELT

HOOK: Kamasan B175, size 10–14
THREAD: Blood red
TAIL: Golden pheasant tippets
BODY: Silver holographic tinsel
WING: White rabbit fur
CHEEKS: Jungle cock
HEAD: Blood red thread

This is best fished in winter on a floating line with short sharp retrieves followed by a long pause.

Tied by Peter Coulson

WATER RAT SMELT

HOOK: Tiemco 5262, size 6–12
THREAD: Black
TAIL: Olive cock hackle fibre and teal feather fibre
BODY: Water rat underfur substitute
RIB: Fine silver wire
THROAT: Mixture olive, orange and teal feather fibre
CHEEKS: Pearl tinsel
HEAD: Black tying thread

Best fished June to October. Experiment with different depths and retrieve speeds—short pulls, jerks, lifting the rod—generally keep the fly moving.

Tied by David Dodd

WESTERN LAKES WANDERER

HOOK: Wet fly 2X long, size 6–10
THREAD: Black 6/0
TAIL: Small clump of tan squirrel tail
BODY: Olive grey chenille
WING: 3 short clumps of black mole fur
HEAD: Black thread

This is a great smelt pattern for the lakes of western Victoria. Best cast in front of smelting fish and retrieved with a smooth figure-of-eight. Most takes are very soft, so be alert.

Tied by Peter Coulson

CHAPTER 18

SPINNERS

BLACK SPINNER (DODD)

HOOK: Kamasan B401, size 12–14
THREAD: Black
TAIL: Good quality paintbrush fibres, tied trident
BODY: Black seal's fur and rabbit blend, lightly dubbed
RIB: Fine silver wire
THORAX: Lightly dubbed black fur
HACKLE: Black cock

Tied by David Dodd

BLACK SPINNER

HOOK: Kamasan B401, size 12–14
THREAD: Black
TAIL: Black cock fibres
BODY: Black thread
RIB: Fine silver wire
HACKLE: Black cock

Tied by Peter Coulson

BIOT SPINNER

HOOK: Dry fly, size 10–16
THREAD: Black
TAIL: Three brown MicroFiBetts
BODY: Black thread
THORAX: Natural C.D.C.
WING: Two white turkey biots

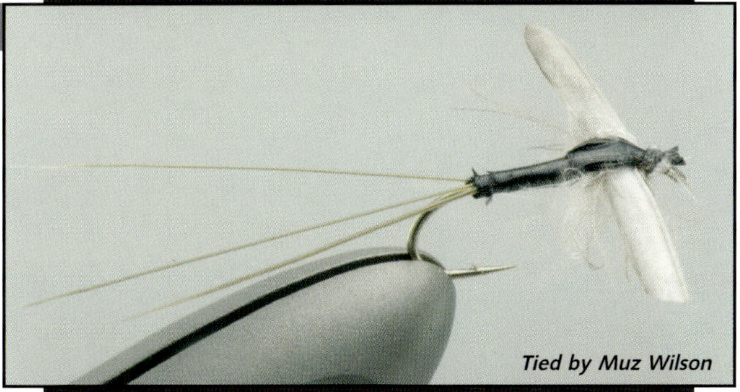

Tied by Muz Wilson

CLOYNE SPINNER

HOOK: Short shank dry fly, size 12–18
THREAD: Black
TAIL & BODY: One hackle feather, colour to suit natural, tied wonderwing fashion. The tail is formed by trimming the hackle stalk and leaving 1–3 barbs on each side.
HACKLE: Cock hackle, colour to match body

Tied by Ezra Bibby

Tied by Noel Jetson

EVENING SPINNER-BLACK

HOOK: Dry fly, size 12–16
THREAD: Black 8/0
TAIL: Dark dun hackle fibres
BODY: Black tying thread
RIB: Fine copper wire
HACKLE: Dark dun, clipped underneath

Tied by Noel Jetson

EVENING SPINNER-ORANGE

HOOK: Dry fly, size 12–16
THREAD: Yellow 8/0
TAIL: Furnace hackle fibres
BODY: Orange silk
RIB: Fine red wire
HACKLE: Dark dun, clipped underneath

Tied by Ezra Bibby

GREEN BIOT

HOOK: Up eye dry, size 12–16
THREAD: Brown 8/0
TAIL: Furnace hackle fibres
BODY: Olive goose biot
HACKLE: Furnace cock

Tied by Lionel Coombs

LIONEL'S SPINNER

HOOK: Dry fly, size 10–16
THREAD: Black
TAIL: Three pheasant tail barbs
BODY: Black thread
HACKLE: Two turns of oversize black cock hackle, tied parachute style

This is an excellent fly to use when polarising fish in the shallows.

ORANGE SPINNER

HOOK: Kamasan B401, size 12–14
THREAD: Orange
TAIL: Buff hackle fibres
BODY: Orange thread
RIB: Fine gold tinsel
HACKLE: Buff cock hackle

Tied by Michael Milczuk

ORANGE SPINNER

HOOK: Kamasan B401, size 12–14
THREAD: Orange
TAIL: Rhode Island Red hackle fibres
BODY: Orange thread
HACKLE: Rhode Island Red cock hackle

Tied by Peter Coulson

PARACHUTE SPINNER

HOOK: Kamasan B401, size 12–18
THREAD: Black
TAIL: Moose hair
BODY: Stripped peacock herl with tip intact to form thorax
POST: Stripped end of hackle post, looped and trimmed
HACKLE: Black cock hackle

Tied by Ezra Bibby

RED SPINNER

HOOK: Kamasan B401, size 12–14
THREAD: Black
TAIL: Good quality paintbrush fibres, tied trident
BODY: Orange seal's fur and rabbit blend, lightly dubbed
RIB: Fine silver wire
THORAX: Lightly dubbed black fur
HACKLE: Red cock

Tied by David Dodd

Tied by Adam Royter

SPENT ANGEL

HOOK: Axisco 070, size 14
THREAD: 6/0 grey
TAIL: Large light blue dun cock hackle
BODY: Light blue dun Antron dubbing
THORAX: Super Fine dubbing, black
WING: Mustad Organza wing, stripped

Good, lightweight, floating wings make this fly perfect for leaving on the water for long periods.

Tied by Peter Coulson

SPENT SPINNER

HOOK: Dry fly, size 10–16
THREAD: Black
TAIL: Two MicroFiBetts
BODY: Black thread
RIB Fine silver wire
WING: White cock hackle fibres, tied in spent style

Tied by Adam Royter

WONDER-GANZA

HOOK: Kamasan B400, size 12
THREAD: Black 6/0
TAIL & BODY: Large black cock hackle
WINGS: Mustad Organza wing
HACKLE: Black cock hackle

This is a good fly for flat water days when the fish are going to get a good look at your fly.

Tied by David Dodd

WONDERWING SPINNER

HOOK: Dry fly, size 12–14
THREAD: Black
TAIL: Black cock hackle
BODY: Black thread
WING: Single hackle feather halved and prepared as wonder wing, then coated with Flexcement
HACKLE: Black cock hackle clipped to form a 'V' underneath

ZING WING SPINNER

HOOK: Dry fly, size 10–16
THREAD: Black
TAIL: Three black micro fibres
BODY: Black thread
WING: Zing wing
HACKLE: Three turns of black cock hackle tied parachute style

GREENWELL SPINNER

HOOK: Kamasan B401, size 12–14
THREAD: White
TAIL: Two pairs of tan MicroFiBetts
BODY: Olive green thread
RIB: Black Monocord
THORAX: Fine pink dubbing
HACKLE: White cock clipped top and bottom

BARB TAIL SPINNER BLACK

HOOK: Kamasan B40, size 12–14
THREAD: Black
TAIL: Two mallard duck fibres
BODY: Black thread
RIB: Fine silver wire
THORAX: Fine red dubbing
HACKLE: Black cock clipped top and bottom

BARB TAIL SPINNER ORANGE

HOOK: Kamasan B401, size 12–14
THREAD: Black
TAIL: Two mallard duck fibres
BODY: Orange thread
RIB: Black Monocord
THORAX: Fine orange dubbing
HACKLE: Fiery brown cock clipped top and bottom

CHAPTER 19

TERRESTRIALS

ADAM ANT

HOOK: Tiemco 200r, size 8–14
THREAD: Black
BODY: Black synthetic dubbing
LEGS: Black rubber

Tied by Adam Royter

ADAM BLACK CICADA

HOOK: Tiemco 200R, size 8–12
THREAD: Black Uni-Thread 6/0
BODY: Spun and clipped black deer hair
WING: Folded white raffia x 2
HEAD: Spun black mink

This is a good fly for the Goulburn River, Victoria, in years when cicadas emerge.

Tied by Adam Royter

ADAM BOGONG

HOOK: Kamasan B175, size 8–10
THREAD: Black
BODY: Cream foam pulled over brown possum dubbing
WING: Two partridge breast feathers
THORAX & LEGS: Teased out brown possum, clipped flat across the bottom

Cast this fly out and leave it. Give it the odd twitch every 30 seconds or so. It works best on flat water in lakes on a moonless night.

Tied by Adam Royter

ADAM CRICKET

HOOK: Tiemco 200r, size 8–10
THREAD: Black
BODY: Black foam
THORAX: Black fine dubbing
LEGS: Dark synthetic raffia knotted
COLLAR: Black deer hair
HEAD: Black deer hair, tied bullet head style

Tied by Adam Royter

Tied by Adam Royter

BEE ROYTED

HOOK: Kamasan B175, size 10
THREAD: Black
TAIL: Black and yellow foam
BODY: Black mink with guard hairs teased out
WING: Light grey cock, tied wonderwing style
EYES: Black plastic bead chain

Tied by David Dodd

BLACK CRICKET

HOOK: Kamasan B401, size 10–12
THREAD: Black
BODY: Black deer hair, spun and clipped to shape
LEGS: Black synthetic raffia, knotted
WING: Black deer hair
HEAD: Black deer hair, tied bullet style

Tied by Adam Royter

BOTSFORD ANT

HOOK: Dry fly, size 18
THREAD: Black 8/0
BODY: Fine black dubbing
WING: Packing sheet foam
HACKLE: Black cock

Tied by Noel Jetson

CORBI MOTH

HOOK: Kamasan B830, size 8
THREAD: Black silk
BODY: Clipped deer hair
WING: Turkey wing
HACKLE: Brown partridge
HEAD: Peacock herl

Originator: Noel Jetson

CRACKENBACK CICADA

HOOK: Tiemco 200r, size 10
THREAD: Black Uni-Thread 6/0
BODY: Green closed cell foam
RIB: Fine pearl tinsel
WING: Two female wood duck breast feathers
COLLAR: Olive green deer hair
HEAD: Olive green deer hair, spun and clipped to shape

EGG & SPIDER

HOOK: Gamakatsu wide gape, size 10
THREAD: Black
EGG: Bean bag ball
BODY: Black foam
THORAX: Black dubbing
LEGS: Knotted black pheasant tail

This fly is best fished in flooded water over new ground.

FUR MOUSE

HOOK: Mustad stinger, wide gape, size 1–8
THREAD: Black
WEEDGUARD: Optional 10 kg mono
UNDERBODY: Closed cell foam, 4 mm sheet
BODY: Cross cut rabbit Zonker strip
TAIL: Soft suede, cut to shape
EARS: Soft suede, cut to shape
HEAD: Rabbit fur, spun in a loop and trimmed to shape
WHISKERS: Deer hair
NOSE: Black thread

FOAM ANT

HOOK: Kamasan B405, size 14–20
THREAD: Black 8/0
BODY: Black foam
HACKLE: Three turns of black cock
HEAD: Black foam

KEAM'S ANT

Tied by Rick Keam

HOOK: Grub hook, size 12–18
THREAD: Black
BODY: Black closed cell foam, tied well back on bend of hook to form a hump
WING: Two narrow lengths of clear white packing string or tan waterproof raffia, twisted once or twice in the middle to form the tip of a flat loop
HACKLE: Black cock hackle, very sparse

MUZ ANT

Tied by Muz Wilson

HOOK: Kamasan B400, size 10–16
THREAD: Black
BODY: Black fine dubbing
UNDERWING: C.D.C. natural grey
WING: Folded Zing wing
HACKLE: Black cock, clipped top and bottom

During an ant hatch cast this fly out and leave it, with the odd twitch. It is also an excellent searching pattern.

NST CICADA

Tied by Adam Royter

HOOK: Kamasan B180, size 4
THREAD: Black Uni-Thread 3/0
TAIL: Red hackle fibres
BODY: Black round foam
RIB: Maxibraid
WING: Pearl flashback, knotted and doubled over lengthways
HEAD & COLLAR: Black deer hair

Cast this fly out and leave it, give it the odd twitch.

PETE'S TERMITE BROWN

Tied by Peter Coulson

HOOK: Kamasan B405, size 14–18
THREAD: Black 6/0
BODY: Fine brown dubbing
WING: Two light grey cock hackle tippets
HACKLE: Three turns of light brown cock
HEAD: Black thread

This fly was originally tied for the Yarra River in Victoria.

PETE'S TERMITE ORANGE

HOOK: Kamasan B405, size 14–18
THREAD: Black 6/0
BODY: Burnt orange floss
WING: Two light grey cock hackle tippets
HACKLE: Three turns of light brown cock
HEAD: Black thread

This fly was originally tied for the Yarra River in Victoria.

PETE'S WASP

HOOK: Dry fly, size 12–16
THREAD: Black 8/0
BODY: Yellow and black ostrich herl
WING: Two grizzle hackle tips
HACKLE: Grizzle cock

PARTRIDGE MOTH

HOOK: Kamasan B405, size 10
THREAD: Black 6/0
BODY: Brown synthetic dubbing
WING: Partridge breast feather
HACKLE: Ginger cock

SIMPLE BLACK CRICKET

HOOK: Tiemco 200r, size 10–8
THREAD: Black Uni-Thread 6/0
BODY: Black seal's fur dubbing
WING: Black deer hair
HEAD: Black deer hair, spun and clipped to shape

Tied by Adam Royter

SIK-ADA

HOOK: Tiemco 200R, size 6–10
THREAD: Olive green Uni-Thread 6/0
BUTT: Orange Sparkleflash
BODY: Olive green synthetic dubbing teased out
RIB: Pearl Slinky Fibre
UNDERWING: Fantastic Wing
HEAD & OVERWING: Olive deer hair
EYES: Black plastic eyes

Cast out and leave this fly, give it the odd strip every 30 seconds or so.

Tied by Andrew Lines

THE YARRA TERMITE

HOOK: Down eye, short shank dry fly, size 14–16
THREAD: Yellow waxed mono cord
BODY: Thin strip of florist tear ribbon
WING: Small bunch of light brown calf tail fibres
HACKLE: Honey or Cree cock

This is a great summer dry fly pattern, especially on hot humid afternoons. Fish this pattern on 1 kg tippet and if nothing is rising cast the fly into the shadows of overhanging foliage or bubble lines.

Tied by Peter Coulson

GREY BOGONG

HOOK: Kamasan B405, size 8–12
THREAD: Black 6/0
TAIL: Grizzle hackle fibres
BODY HACKLE: Grizzle cock
WING: Two guinea fowl feathers
HACKLE: Grizzle cock

Tied by Adam Royter

YARRA THUNDER ANT

HOOK: Kamasan 401, size 16
THREAD: Black 8/0
BODY: Light tan dubbing
WING: Two natural C.D.C.
HACKLE: Light brown cock clipped at the bottom

This is one of the best flies for flat water termite fishing. It was originally tied for the Yarra River in Victoria.

STRINGWING CICADA

HOOK: Tiemco 2312, size 14–6
THREAD: Bug Thread or other stout synthetic
BODY: Dyed kangaroo or other air-retentive fur clipped straight from hide, thickly spun in a dubbing loop, densely wrapped then trimmed to shape
WINGS: Each formed from a length of bright clear-white waterproof packing string, twice-twisted or knotted in the middle and returned on itself to form a flat loop

Tied by Rick Keam

CHAPTER 20

TOM JONES & BAG FLIES

BEAD HEAD TOM JONES

HOOK: Kamasan B175, size 10–12, straighten the eye
THREAD: Black
TAIL: Black cock hackle fibres
BODY: Olive dubbing blend
WING: Teased out dubbing
RIB: Gold wire
HEAD: Gold bead

With the addition of a bead this Tom Jones swims completely differently to and deeper than the normal pattern. This pattern works really well in the tails of runs.

Tied by Peter Coulson

CRYSTAL TOM

HOOK: Kamasan B175, size 10–16
THREAD: Black
TAIL: Hare's mask with guard hairs, dyed olive
BELLY: Krystal Flash
WING: Three very small clumps of hare's mask with guard hairs, dyed olive
HEAD: Black tying thread

Tied by Peter Coulson

DIRTY TOM

HOOK: Kamasan B175, size 6–12
THREAD: Black
TAIL: Large clump of dark brown beaver
BODY: Olive dubbing blend
WING: Two large clumps of olive hare's fur
RIB: Fine copper wire
THROAT: Olive cock hackle fibres

This is a good pattern for dirty water—it has a large profile and moves a lot of water with each strip.

Tied by Peter Coulson

GOLDEN TOM JONES

HOOK: Kamasan B175, size 10–14
THREAD: Black
TAIL: Olive rabbit
BODY: Gold tinsel
WING: Olive rabbit

This fly works well for lake and river fishing when tied 300 mm behind a larger attractor fly.

Tied by Peter Coulson

GREEN FOX

Tied by Michael Milczuk

HOOK: X-long, size 10–6
THREAD: Black
TAIL: Fox tail
BODY: Olive chenille
WING: Fox tail, in two sections

KANGAROO FLY

Tied by Michael Milczuk

HOOK: X-long, size 12–6
THREAD: Yellow
TAIL: Grey kangaroo fur
WING: Grey kangaroo fur

PEARL JONES

Tied by Peter Coulson

HOOK: Long shank, straight eye, size 6–12
THREAD: Black
TAIL: Dark olive cock hackle fibres
BODY: Olive dubbing blend overwrapped with pearl tinsel
WING: Two very small clumps of kangaroo

This variation is great for smelting fish on dull days in the western lakes of Victoria.

SILVER JONES

Tied by Peter Coulson

HOOK: Kamasan B175, size 10–16
THREAD: Black
TAIL: Black cock hackle fibres
BODY: Silver oval tinsel
WING: Two clumps of olive beaver fur

SPARKLE TOM

HOOK: Kamasan B175, size 10–16
THREAD: Black
TAIL: Hare's mask with guard hairs, dyed olive
BODY: Olive dubbing blend
THROAT: Krystal Flash
WING: Three very small clumps of hare's mask with guard hairs, dyed olive
HEAD: Black tying thread

Tied by Peter Coulson

TOM JONES (Coulson)

HOOK: Kamasan B175, size 10–16
THREAD: Black
TAIL: Black cock hackle fibres
BODY: Olive dubbing blend
WING: Two very small clumps of olive beaver fur
TAG: Red floss

My variation of John Lanchester's original red-tagged Tom Jones, with the kangaroo fur replaced by beaver fur. This was tied in as an attractor and works very well on smelting fish. It is best fished very slowly on a floating line cast into the middle of smelting fish.

Tied by Peter Coulson

TOM JONES (Dodd)

HOOK: Kamasan B830, size 8–10
THREAD: Black
TAIL: Black squirrel tail
UNDERBODY: Lead or copper wire (optional)
BODY: Olive dyed lambs wool or kangaroo belly fur (summer coat is best)
WINGS: Kangaroo belly fur, dyed olive
RIB: Flat copper wire
THROAT: Olive cock fibre

Tied by David Dodd

TOM JONES PARTRIDGE

HOOK: Partridge style, up eye, size 10–16
THREAD: Black
BUT: Gold tinsel
TAIL: Black cock hackle fibres
BODY: Olive dubbing blend
WING: Two very small clumps of olive beaver fur
RIB: Fine embossed gold tinsel
TAG: Red floss

Tied by Peter Coulson

TOM JONES PEARL

Tied by Peter Coulson

HOOK: Kamasan B175, size 10–12, straighten the eye
THREAD: Black
TAIL: Dark olive cock hackle fibres
BODY: Olive dubbing blend
WING: Teased out dubbing
RIB: Pearl tinsel

This variation is great for smelting fish. Cast the fly well ahead of the smelting fish then retrieve with a slow figure-of-eight motion.

TOM JONES (Rees)

Tied by Stuart Rees

HOOK: Kamasan B175, size 8–16
THREAD: Dark olive green
TAIL: Black mink
BODY: Olive dubbing blend
WING: Two very small clumps of olive rabbit's fur
RIB: Copper wire

There is no doubt the Tom Jones as I tie it represents smelt, stick caddis, nymphs and scud. The only factor determining the identity is the retrieve, fast for smelt, slow for stick caddis or nymphs and dead still for scud. *Originator: John Lanchester*

UPSIDEDOWN TOM JONES

Tied by Peter Coulson

HOOK: Kamasan B175, size 10–12
THREAD: Black
TAIL: Black cock hackle fibres
UNDERBODY: Lead wire tied on top of the hook shank
BODY: Olive dubbing blend
WING: Dark olive rabbit
RIB: Fine gold wire

This is an excellent fly to fish around weeds as it swims hook point up.

BAG FLY (COULSON)

Tied by Peter Coulson

HOOK: Kamasan B175, size 8–10
TAIL: Black squirrel tail
BODY: Gold tinsel
RIB: Fine gold oval wire
WING: Hemp fibre
OVERWING: Black squirrel tail
THROAT: Red hackle fibres

BAG FLY (HILL)

HOOK: Kamasan B175, size 10–14
TAIL: Black squirrel tail
BODY: Gold tinsel
RIB: Fine gold wire
WING: Green wallaby
OVERWING: Orange hackle fibres
THROAT: Black hackle fibres

This is best fished down and across in fast water.

Tied by James Hill

BAG FLY CRYSTAL

HOOK: Long shank, size 8–14
TAIL: Black squirrel tail
BODY: Fine gold tinsel
OVERWING: Orange hackle fibres
WING: Hemp fibre
UNDERWING: Krystal Flash
THROAT: Black hackle fibres

This fly is best fished down and across in fast water or fast stripped in lakes.

Tied by Peter Coulson

BAG FLY

HOOK: Kamasan B175, size 10–14
THREAD: Black
TAIL: Hemp fibre
BODY: Hemp fibres
RIB: Embossed flat gold tinsel
HEAD: Black thread
TYING NOTES: Body is wrapped forward, then remainder laid back over to form back and tail, secured with the rib.

Tied by Peter Coulson

BAG FLY MINI

HOOK: Kamasan B175, size 12–14
TAIL: Black squirrel tail
BODY: Gold tinsel
RIB: Fine gold oval wire
WING: Hemp fibre
OVERWING: Black squirrel tail
THROAT: Orange hackle fibres

This fly is best fished fast to very fast in rivers.

Tied by Peter Coulson

CHAPTER 21

WETS

007 WET

HOOK: Kamasan B175, size 10–14
THREAD: Black
TAIL: Hot pink Antron
BODY: Blue tinsel
RIB: Fine silver wire
WING: Black squirrel tail
HACKLE: Black hen
CHEEKS: Jungle cock, red
HEAD: Black thread

A good middle dropper fly generally fished as an attractor when fishing a team of wets.

Tied by Peter Coulson

ADANDRA

HOOK: Wet, size 10
THREAD: Black 6/0
TAIL: Red marabou
BODY: Silver lurex and round silver tinsel
OVERWING: Peacock breast feathers
THROAT HACKLE: Black hen hackle fibres
EYES: Jungle cock
HEAD: varnish finished with holographic glitter

Fish this on a floating or intermediate line with a strip, pause retrieve for rainbow trout. Also known as 'The new stocky special ' because of its ability to catch lots of freshly stocked rainbow trout.

Tied by Adam Royter

ADANDRA 11

HOOK: Wet, size 10
THREAD: Black 6/0
TAIL: Red HIVIS
BODY: Silver lurex and round silver tinsel
WING: Peacock breast feathers
THROAT HACKLE: Dark blue hen hackle fibres
HEAD: Black

Tied by Adam Royter

BEADHEAD WET

HOOK: Kamasan B175, size 10–14
THREAD: Black
TAIL: Olive marabou
BODY: Olive dubbing mix
WINGS: Pheasant rump feathers
THORAX: Tan Antron dubbing, picked out
HEAD: Powder coated brass bead

Tied by Adam Royter

Tied by Adam Royter

BEC'S RAINBOW FLY

HOOK: Kamasan 830, size 4–8
THREAD: Black 6/0
HEAD: Glass bead, pearl
BODY: Yellow, orange, red, hot pink and purple marabou
COLLAR: Purple SLF dubbing

A good fly for annoying large lake trout. Bright, nasty and in their face. It also works well after dark.

Tied by Peter Coulson

BLACK BETTY

HOOK: Kamasan B175, size 4–10
THREAD: Black
TAIL: Black marabou
BODY: Fine black dubbing
HACKLE: Two turns of black cock
EYES: Chrome plated dumbbell eyes

This fly was developed to represent stone flies in big, fast rivers.

Tied by Peter Coulson

BLACK & SILVER

HOOK: Kamasan B175, size 10–12
THREAD: Black
TAIL: Black squirrel tail
BODY: Silver tinsel
COLLAR: Black squirrel tail
HEAD: Black

Tied by Peter Coulson

BLEEDIN' WET

HOOK: Kamasan B175, size 10–14
THREAD: Black
TAIL: Black hackle fibres
BODY: Two thirds black at the rear and a third red seal's fur dubbing
RIB: Fine silver oval tinsel
WING: Black hackle fibres
HACKLE: Black hen
CHEEKS: Jungle cock, red
HEAD: Black thread

A good middle dropper fly when fishing a team of wets.

BORGIES GREEN THING

HOOK: Kamasan B830, size 10–14
THREAD: Green
TAIL: Black marabou
BODY: Green Crystal chenille
RIB: Green ostrich herl
WEIGHT: Optional lead wire

Fish this fly in lakes in tandem with small wets and nymphs. Small Green Things, sizes 12 and 14 with gold bead heads work well fished in rivers. *Originator: Matt Borg*

Tied by Matt Borg

HELTER SMELTER

HOOK: Tiemco 5263, sizes 10, 8
THREAD: Olive or black
TAIL: Short bunch of hackle fluff from feather duster, natural or dyed olive
BODY: Light olive green Antron or natural dubbing teased well out for translucency, with a single strand of pearl Krystal Flash angling back on each side, secured at the front
THROAT: Danville's Flat Waxed Nylon fluorescent red, lightly varnished
HEAD: Bright yellow-green Maria George 8/0 glass Seed Bead, shade 18

Tied by Rick Keam

BREDBO WITH UNDERWING

HOOK: Wet fly, size 10–16
THREAD: Black 8/0
TAIL: Red cock fibres
BODY: Orange silk
RIB: Fine gold wire
WING: Speckled turkey tail slips
UNDERWING: Golden pheasant tippets
THROAT: Dark brown hen hackle
HEAD: Tying thread

Tied by Michael Milczuk

BUTCHER

HOOK: Kamasan B175, size10–14
THREAD: Black 8/0
BODY: Silver tinsel
RIB: Fine silver wire
WING: Peacock breast feather
THROAT: Black hen hackle
HEAD: Tying thread

This is best fished down and across in rivers.

Tied by Peter Coulson

Tied by Peter Coulson

COACHMAN

HOOK: Wet fly, size 12–16
THREAD: Black
BUTT: Flat gold tinsel
BODY: Peacock herl
WING: White duck wing quill sections
THROAT HACKLE: Fiery brown cock, laid back
HEAD: Tying thread

Tied by Andrew Lines

DLC SPECIAL

HOOK: Long down eye, size 10
THREAD: Black or yellow
BODY: Fluorescent yellow, fine fibre, polyester sash cord
TAIL: Same as body, Baby Doll-style
COLLAR: Fluorescent orange, fine fibre, polyester sash cord

Fish this fly on sinking or sink tip line with quick jerky retrieve and pause.

Tied by Ezra Bibby

FUR FLY VARIANT

HOOK: Kamasan B220, size 6–10
THREAD: Brown
BODY: Rabbit fur dubbing brush, formed with fine red wire and natural rabbit fur
WING: Natural rabbit fur Zonker strip
HEAD: Peacock herl

Tied by Noel Jetson

FLASHY TRUGANINI

HOOK: Salmon style wet fly hook, size 6–10
THREAD: Black 8/0
BODY: Red floss along back, wrapped with pearl Flashabou
TAG: Red floss
WING: Black hen hackle fibres
HEAD: Peacock herl, lacquered

FUZZY WUZZY

HOOK: Kamasan B830, size 6–10
THREAD: Black
TAIL: Black squirrel tail
UNDERBODY: Lead or copper wire (optional)
BODY: Red chenille
HACKLE: Black hen
TYING NOTE: Body colours that also work well are olive, black, brown, orange and yellow

Tied by David Dodd

FUZZY WUZZY BLACK RABBIT

HOOK: Kamasan, size 8–12
THREAD: Yellow 6/0
TAIL: Black cock fibres
BODY: Silver flat tinsel
COLLAR: Black rabbit
HEAD: Yellow thread

Tied by Peter Coulson

FUZZY WUZZY DARK AQUA

HOOK: Kamasan B830, size 6–10
THREAD: Black
TAIL: Dark aqua cock fibres
RIB: Green copper wire
UNDERBODY: Lead or copper wire (optional)
BODY: Dark aqua dubbing
HACKLE: Dark aqua cock fibres

Tied by Peter Coulson

FUZZY WUZZY PURPLE

HOOK: Kamasan, size 2–8
THREAD: Black
TAIL: Black squirrel tail, long
BODY: Purple wool
HACKLE: Long black cock neck hackle

Tied by Peter Coulson

FUZZY WUZZY RED

HOOK: Kamasan, size 2–8
THREAD: Black
TAIL: Black squirrel tail, long
BODY: Red wool
HACKLE: Long black cock neck hackle

GOLD & BLACK

HOOK: Kamasan, size 10–14
THREAD: Black
TAIL: Black marabou
BODY: Gold tinsel
RIB: Fine copper wire
WING: Black marabou
HEAD: Brass bead to suit hook size

Best fished as point fly in lakes.

GREEN EYED MONSTER

HOOK: Mustad 34007, size 4–10
THREAD: Chartreuse
TAIL: Purple marabou
BODY: Black marabou
HEAD: Tying thread
EYES: Chartreuse stick on
TYING NOTE: Head and eyes are covered in a light coat of epoxy.

Fish on a sinking or intermediate line. Cast to structure and let sink to required depth. Retrieve with very short strips and twitches, keeping the fly in the strike zone for as long as possible.

HAMILL'S KILLER

HOOK: Kamasan B830, size 4–10
THREAD: Black
TAIL: Black squirrel tail with golden pheasant tippet on top
UNDERBODY: Lead or copper wire (optional)
BODY: Red, olive or yellow wool
WINGS: Grey partridge feathers dyed olive, tied Killer style

LIMELIGHT

HOOK: Long shank, size 4–10
THREAD: Red
TAIL: Dyed bright green pheasant rump feathers
UNDERBODY: Lead or copper wire (optional)
BODY: Lime green chenille
WINGS: Three bunches of three dyed bright green pheasant rump feathers
HEAD: Red

This fly is best fished with long strips in lakes during the colder months.

Tied by Peter Coulson

MAGGOT FLY

HOOK: Down eye, size 14
THREAD: Black mono cord
BODY: Four or five pearl coloured glass beads

This fly fishes well where maggots are commonly used as bait and is best fished under a dry fly or indicator.

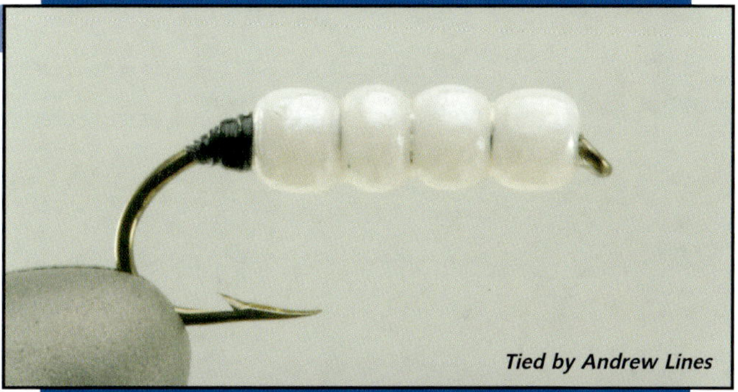

Tied by Andrew Lines

MALLARD AND CLARET

HOOK: Wet fly, size 10–16
THREAD: Black
TAIL: Golden pheasant tippets
BODY: Claret seal's fur
RIB: Fine gold wire
WING: Bronze mallard
THROAT: Furnace cock hackle fibres

Tied by Michael Milczuk

MALLARD AND BROWN

HOOK: Kamasan B175, size 10–16
THREAD: Red
TAIL: Mallard breast feather fibres
BODY: Brown seal's fur
RIB: Fine gold wire
BODY HACKLE: Fiery brown cock, laid back
HEAD HACKLE: Mallard duck swept back
HEAD: Tying thread

Tied by Peter Coulson

Tied by Adam Royter

MORNING GLORY

HOOK: Black Magic 8–10
THREAD: Black 6/0
TAIL: Olive hackle fibres
RIBBING: Silver holographic Flashabou
DUBBING: Peacock green Scintilla
OVERWING: Peacock chest feather
THROAT: Wood duck chest feathers
COLLAR HACKLE: Hot pink saddle

This fly is the traditional style of wet that doesn't imitate anything in pa ular and is a good fly for both brown and rainbow trout, doing its best in the morning.

Tied by David Dodd

MRS SIMPSON

HOOK: Kamasan B830, size 4–10
THREAD: Black
TAIL: Black squirrel tail
UNDERBODY: Lead or copper wire (optional)
BODY: Red or yellow wool or chenille
WINGS: Pheasant rump feathers, tied Killer style

Tied by Peter Coulson

MRS SIMPSON BROWN

HOOK: Kamasan B830, size 4–10
THREAD: Black
TAIL: Black squirrel tail
UNDERBODY: Lead or copper wire (optional)
BODY: Yellow wool
WINGS: Dyed brown pheasant rump feathers, tied Killer style

Tied by Michael Milczuk

MURDOCH

HOOK: Wet fly, size 10–16
THREAD: Black
TAG: Fine silver wire
TAIL: Mallard flank fibres
BODY: Grey possum fur
WING: Ringneck pheasant back feather
THROAT: Scarlet hen hackle fibres

OLIVE FUR FLY

HOOK: Kamasan B175, size 8–12
THREAD: Olive
TAG: Red wool
WING: Olive rabbit fur Zonker strip
HEAD: Olive ostrich herl

Tied by Peter Coulson

PALMER HACKLE BLACK

HOOK: Axisco 730, size 8–12
THREAD: Black 6/0
BODY: Black ostrich herl
RIB: Fine gold tinsel
HACKLE: Black cock or hen tied palmer style
HEAD: Black thread

Tied by Mick Hall

PALMER HACKLE BROWN

HOOK: Axisco 730, size 8–12
THREAD: Black 6/0
BODY: Deep amber mohair
RIB: Fine gold tinsel
HACKLE: Natural red cock or hen tied palmer style
HEAD: Black thread

Tied by Mick Hall

PALMER HACKLE GOLDEN

HOOK: Axisco 730, size 8–12
THREAD: Green 6/0
BODY: Gold peacock herl
RIB: Gold tinsel
HACKLE: Bright red cock or hen tied palmer style
HEAD: Black thread

Tied by Mick Hall

PALMER HACKLE PEACOCK

HOOK: Axisco 730, size 8–12
THREAD: Red 6/0
BODY: Good quality peacock herl
RIB: Silver tinsel
HACKLE: Dark grizzle cock or hen tied palmer style
HEAD: Scarlet mohair

PALMER HACKLE ORANGE & BLA

HOOK: Axisco 730, size 8–12
THREAD: Black 6/0
TAGS: White floss teased out each end of the hook
BODY: Black and orange chenille
HACKLE: Grizzle cock or hen tied palmer style
HEAD: Black thread

PALMER HACKLE RED

HOOK: Axisco 730, size 8–12
THREAD: Bright red 6/0
BODY: Dark red mohair
RIB: Gold tinsel
HACKLE: Natural red cock or hen tied palmer style
HEAD: Bright red thread

PALMERED MARCH BROWN

HOOK: Kamasan B175, size 10–12
THREAD: Black or brown
TAIL: Mustard coloured wool
BODY: Hare's fur
RIB: Gold flat tinsel
BODY HACKLE: Palmered red hen
HEAD HACKLE: Partridge

This is generally used as an emerger with a team of flies.

PALMER (WET)

HOOK: Kamasan B175, size 8–20
THREAD: Black 6/0
TAIL: Red cock hackle fibres
BODY: Black floss
BODY HACKLE: Palmered black hen

Tied by Michael Milczuk

PARTRIDGE AND ORANGE

HOOK: Kamasan B405, size 10–16
THREAD: Black 6/0
BODY: Hot orange floss
HACKLE: Brown partridge breast feather
HEAD: Black thread

Tied by Mick Hall

PEACOCK AND BLACK

HOOK: Kamasan B405, size 12–14
THREAD: Black
TAG: Yellow wool (optional)
BODY: Peacock herl
HACKLE: Black

A simple hackled wet fly that dates back to the days of early fly tying.

Tied by David Dodd

PEACOCK HAMILL'S

HOOK: 2X long, size 4–10
THREAD: Black
TAIL: Black squirrel tail with golden pheasant tippet on top
BODY: Red, olive or yellow wool
WINGS: Peacock breast feathers tied Killer style
THROAT: Red cock fibres
CHEEKS: Jungle cock
HEAD: Black

Tied by Peter Coulson

Tied by Peter Coulson

PETER RABBIT REDFIN

HOOK: Partridge Wilson Salmon, size 6
THREAD: Black
TAIL: Black rabbit
BODY: Yellow under black rabbit with red throat tied in clumps along hook shank.
HEAD: Black

This is a great winter attractor pattern for both rivers and lakes. The retri should be fast and erratic.

Tied by Peter Coulson

PETER RABBIT RED & BLACK

HOOK: Partridge Wilson Salmon, size 6
THREAD: Black
TAIL: Black rabbit
BODY: Red and black rabbit tied in clumps and spun around the hook shank.
HEAD: Black

This is a great winter attractor pattern for both rivers and lakes. The retr should be fast and erratic.

Tied by Peter Coulson

PETER RABBIT SUNSET

HOOK: Partridge Wilson Salmon, size 6
THREAD: Black
TAIL: Black rabbit
BODY: Black, yellow and orange rabbit tied in clumps and spun around the hook shank.
HEAD: Black and yellow

This is a great winter attractor pattern for both rivers and lakes. The retrieve should be fast and erratic.

Tied by Peter Coulson

PETER RABBIT YELLOW & BLACK

HOOK: Partridge Wilson Salmon, size 6
THREAD: Black
TAIL: Black rabbit
BODY: Yellow and black rabbit tied in clumps and spu around the hook shank.
HEAD: Black

This is a great winter attractor pattern for both rivers and lakes. The ret should be fast and erratic.

PINK PERIL

HOOK: Kamasan B405, size 6–12
THREAD: Red Uni-Thread 6/0
TAIL: Golden pheasant tippets
BODY: Hot pink chenille
RIB: Fine red tinsel
WING: Black rabbit Zonker tied in matuka style

Tied by Roger Butler

PONDAGE FLY GOLD

HOOK: Kamasan B405, size 10
THREAD: Black Uni-Thread 6/0
EYES: Medium gold bead-chain
BODY: Tying thread
RIB: Gold holographic ShimmerFlash, fine
TAIL: Gold holographic ShimmerFlash, fine

Cast long and allow the fly to sink to the required depth. Retrieve with long steady strips, alternating fast and slow.

Tied by Rod Groaters

PONDAGE FLY SILVER

HOOK: Kamasan B405, size 10
THREAD: Black Uni-Thread 6/0
EYES: Medium silver bead-chain
BODY: Tying thread
RIB: Silver holographic ShimmerFlash, fine
TAIL: Silver holographic ShimmerFlash, fine

Cast long and allow the fly to sink to the required depth. Retrieve with long steady strips, alternating fast and slow strips.

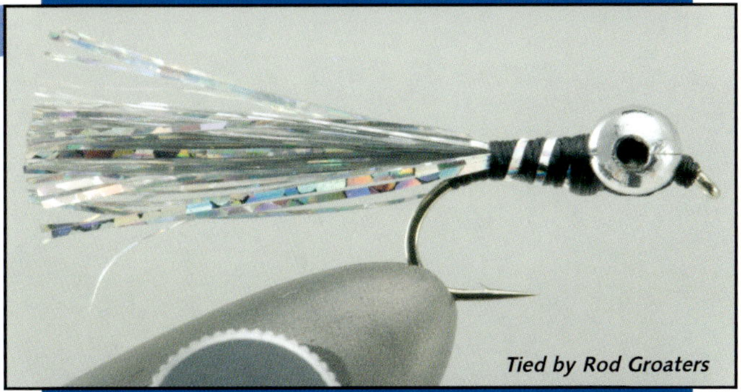
Tied by Rod Groaters

RED AND GRIZZLE

HOOK: Wet fly size 8–10
THREAD: Black
TAIL: Red marabou
BODY: Palmered aftershaft feather, and grizzle hackle feather

Tied by Michael Milczuk

Tied by Peter Coulson

ROBIN'S FLY

HOOK: Kamasan B175, size 8–12
THREAD: Black 6/0
TAIL: Black squirrel tail
BODY: Metallic blue craft thread
CHEEKS: Jungle cock
WING: Red marabou
HEAD: Black thread

This fly is best fished down and across in small rivers.

Tied by Peter Coulson

ROYAL COACHMAN

HOOK: Wet fly, size 10–16
THREAD: Black
TAIL: Golden pheasant tippets
BODY: Peacock herl, red floss, peacock herl
WING: White duck wing quill sections
THROAT HACKLE: Fiery brown cock, laid back
HEAD: Tying thread

Tied by Peter Coulson

SCOTCH POACHER

HOOK: Kamasan B175, Size 6–10
THREAD: Black
TAIL: Bunch of black squirrel tail (long)
BODY: Dubbed orange seal's fur
WING: Three or four pukeko breast feathers
CHEEKS: Jungle cock

The retrieve should be slow with the odd quick strip then pause for abou seconds. This fly fishes well at all depths.

Tied by Peter Coulson

SOFT HACKLE SNAIL

HOOK: Kamasan B175, size 10–12
THREAD: Black 6/0
BODY: Peacock herl
HACKLE: Duck breast feather swept back
HEAD: Black thread

This fly is best fished in lakes with a heave and leave retrieve, with the odd metre strip.

SOFT HACKLE SPINNER BLACK

HOOK: Kamasan B405, size 10–16
THREAD: Black 6/0
BODY: Super fine black dubbing
HACKLE: Two turns of black hen
HEAD: Black thread

This is a great pattern for down and across fishing in small rivers in the middle of the day. At the end of the swing, wiggle the rod tip slightly to entice a take.

Tied by Peter Coulson

SOFT HACKLE SPINNER ORANGE

HOOK: Kamasan B405, size 10–16
THREAD: Black 6/0
BODY: Burnt orange synthetic dubbing
THORAX: Fine brown synthetic dubbing
HACKLE: Two turns of light brown mottled grouse
HEAD: Black thread

Tied by Mick Hall

SPIDER GREEN

HOOK: Kamasan B830, size 12–14
THREAD: Grey
BODY: Green tinsel
THORAX: Green dubbing
HACKLE: Black hen

This fly is best fished down and across in rivers pre-hatches.

Tied by Peter Coulson

SPIDER PINK

HOOK: Kamasan B830, size 12–14
THREAD: Grey
BODY: Pink tinsel
THORAX: Pink dubbing
HACKLE: Black hen

This fly is best fished down and across in rivers pre-hatches.

Tied by Peter Coulson

Tied by David Dodd

SUNSET BUMBLE

HOOK: Kamasan B175, size 10–12
THREAD: Black
TAIL: Red wool
BODY: Red dubbing
BODY HACKLE: Palmered red and orange hackle
HEAD HACKLE: Black

A good candidate for a middle dropper fly and generally fished as an attractor when fishing a team of wets.

Tied by David Dodd

SUNSET FLY

HOOK: Tiemco 5262, size 6–10
THREAD: Yellow
TAIL: Black squirrel
HACKLE: Rear third bright yellow, middle third hot orange, front black cock
HEAD HACKLE: Black and yellow tying thread

Cast the fly out and allow it to sink for 5–20 seconds then retrieve with steady pulls.

Tied by Peter Coulson

SUNSET RABBIT FUR

HOOK: Kamasan B175, size 10
THREAD: Black
TAIL: Black squirrel tail
BODY: Yellow, orange and black rabbit tied in clumps and spun around the hook shank.
HEAD: Black and yellow

Tied by Noel Jetson

TADS

HOOK: Dry fly, size 10–16
THREAD: Black 8/0
BODY: Mixture of maroon and black seal's fur dubbing
TAIL: Black hen hackle fibres
THROAT: Light brown possum dubbing
HACKLE: Black hen, one or two turns only
HEAD: Black thread

WEE PETER

HOOK: Dry fly, size 14–16
THREAD: Black
BODY: Rear two-thirds flat silver tinsel, front third red fluorescent wool
HACKLE: One turn of black hen hackle

Fish this fly as part of a team of wets.

WATSON'S FANCY

HOOK: Kamasan B175, size 10–14
THREAD: Black
BUTT: Red floss
TAIL: Golden pheasant crest
BODY: Back half red, front half black seals' fur dubbing
RIB: Fine silver wire
WING: Starling tied wet style
HACKLE: Black hen
CHEEKS: Jungle cock
HEAD: Black thread

A good middle dropper fly fished as an attractor when fishing a team of wets. This fly also works well in the shallows in winter on its own.

WILLIAMSON'S SNOWY MOUNTAINS GOLDFISH

HOOK: Mustad limerick 3666, size 6–10
THREAD: Yellow or fluorescent yellow
INNER WING: Gold marabou with pearl Krystal Flash
OUTER WING: Yellow mallard flank
HEAD: Black thread

WOOLLY WORM BLACK

HOOK: Kamasan, size 8–12
THREAD: Black 6/0
BODY: Fine black chenille
RIB: Gold tinsel
HACKLE: Black cock or hen tied palmer style
HEAD: Black thread

Tied by Bruce Gibson

WOOLHEAD BLACK & GOLD

HOOK: Kamasan B175, size 6
THREAD: Black
BODY & TAIL: Gold Maxibraid
WING: Black rabbit Zonker
HEAD: Black Mara wool spun and clipped

Tied by Bruce Gibson

WOOLHEAD BLACK & PEACOCK

HOOK: Kamasan B175, size 6
THREAD: Black
BODY & TAIL: Peacock Maxibraid
WING: Black rabbit Zonker
HEAD: Black Mara wool spun and clipped

Tied by Ezra Bibby

WOOLLY WORM GREEN GRIZZLE

HOOK: Wet, size 8–12
THREAD: Black 6/0
TAG: Bright green HIVIS
BODY: Dark green dubbing
RIB: Fine silver wire
HACKLE: Dyed green grizzle tied palmer style
HEAD: Black thread

Tied by Mick Hall

WOOLLY WORM (HALL)

HOOK: Axisco 730, size 8–12
THREAD: Black 6/0
TAG: Red wool
BODY: Olive green chenille
RIB: Gold tinsel
HACKLE: Black cock or hen tied palmer style
HEAD: Black thread

Y2K

HOOK: Kamasan B175, size 10
THREAD: Black
BODY: Brown olive SLF dubbing
RIB: Gold round tinsel
WING: Olive kangaroo
CHEEKS: White rabbit
THROAT: Red rabbit
HEAD: Dubbed olive kangaroo

This is best fished on a floating line in lakes during the summer months. All retrieves work with this pattern.

Tied by Daryl Grant

YETI BLACK & GREEN

HOOK: Kamasan B175, size 8
THREAD: Black
BUTT: Fluorescent green chenille
BODY: Black chenille
RIB: Gold wire
WING: Black mink Zonker
HEAD: Black

Tied by Bruce Gibson

YETI BLACK & RED

HOOK: Kamasan B175, size 8
THREAD: Black
BUTT: Fluorescent red chenille
BODY: Black chenille
RIB: Gold wire
WING: Black mink Zonker
HEAD: Black

Tied by Bruce Gibson

ZULU

HOOK: Wet fly, size 12–16
THREAD: Black
TAG: Red wool
BODY: Black ostrich herl, palmered with black cock hackle
RIB: Gold flat tinsel
HACKLE: Black cock hackle

Tied by Michael Milczuk

CHAPTER 22

WOOLLY BUGGERS

ESTAZ WOOLLY BUGGER

HOOK: Size 6–12 long
THREAD: Black
TAIL: Black under purple marabou with six strands of black holographic tinsel
BODY: Gold Estaz chenille
HACKLE: Large black cock, palmer style
HEAD: Black

This is best fished fast to very fast in lakes. It can be fished at all depths.

FLASH HARRY

HOOK: Kamasan B175, size 4–10
THREAD: Black
TAIL: Black marabou extra long with ten strands of pearl tinsel
BODY: Black dubbing
HACKLE: Black cock, palmer style
HEAD: Brass bead

This is best fished extra fast in lakes.

FLASH HARRY (COOMBS)

HOOK: Kamasan B175, size 4–10
THREAD: Black
TAIL: Black marabou extra long with ten strands of silver holographic tinsel
BODY: Black Estaz chenille
HEAD: Black

This is best fished extra fast in lakes.

FLASHY BUGGER

HOOK: Kamasan B175, size 10–12
THREAD: Red
TAIL: Black marabou extra long with six strands of pearl tinsel
BODY: Lime green synthetic dubbing mix
HACKLE: Grizzle cock, palmer style
HEAD: Red

This is best fished extra fast in lakes

FUZZY BUGGER GREEN

HOOK: Kamasan B175, size 8–12
THREAD: Red
TAIL: Black mink
BODY: Dark green Lure Flash
HACKLE: Black cock hackle, tied palmered

Generally a winter/spring fly the Fuzzy Bugger is best fished slow and deep. Chinook salmon have shown a distinct liking to the fly in Victoria's western lakes.

FUZZY BUGGER BLUE

HOOK: Kamasan B175, size 10–14
THREAD: Black
TAIL: Black cock fibres
BODY: Blue Lure Flash
HACKLE: Black cock hackle, tied palmered

FUZZY BUGGER

HOOK: Kamasan B175, size 10–14
THREAD: Red
TAIL: Black cock fibres
BODY: Dark pearl Lure Flash
HACKLE: Black cock hackle, tied palmered
HEAD: Red

GREENHEAD WOOLLY BUGGER

HOOK: Size 6–12 long
THREAD: Black
TAIL: Black marabou
UNDERBODY: Lead or copper wire (optional)
BODY: Black chenille
HACKLE: Black cock wound from back to the front
HEAD: Green wool

JIG A BUGGER BLACK

HOOK: Kamasan B175, size 6–8
THREAD: Black
TAIL: Black marabou with six strands of pearl Krystal Flash
BODY: Black dubbing
HACKLE: Black cock, palmer style
EYES: Chrome lead dumbbells

This fly is best fished on floating line with a short, quick retrieve followed by a long pause.

Tied by Peter Coulson

JIG A BUGGER ORANGE

HOOK: Kamasan B175, size 6–8
THREAD: Red
TAIL: Hot orange marabou with six strands of orange Krystal Flash
BODY: Pearl Crystal Chenille
HACKLE: Orange cock, palmer style
EYES: Chrome lead dumbbells

This fly is best fished late season on floating line with a short quick retrieve followed by a long pause.

Tied by Peter Coulson

JIG A BUGGER PINK

HOOK: Kamasan B175, size 6–8
THREAD: Red
TAIL: Pink marabou with six strands of pearl Krystal Flash
BODY: Pearl Crystal Chenille
HACKLE: Pink cock, palmer style
HEAD HACKLE: The fluff from large pink cock hackle
EYES: Chrome lead dumbbells

This fly is best fished late season on floating line with a short, quick retrieve followed by a long pause.

Tied by Peter Coulson

JUST RIGHT BUGGER

HOOK: Long shank, size 10–8
THREAD: Black 6/0
TAIL: Light brown and chartreuse marabou with a tuft of red
PALMER HACKLE: Chartreuse grizzly cock hackle
UNDER BODY: Pearl chenille
LEAD: Full shank of 0.20 mm

Fish this fly across and down in the tail out of a fast run at first light in the months after March. This fly is not too heavy, not too light—but just right !!

Tied by Adam Royter

PINK BUGGER

Tied by Daryl Grant

HOOK: Kamasan B175 size 8–10
THREAD: Black
TAIL: Pink Chickabou with pearl Krystal Flash
HACKLE: Pink and black Chickabou
EYES: Bead chain

Fish this pattern on a sink tip line down and across in fast water. This is a good pattern for rainbow trout in the Goulburn River in Victoria.

WOOLLY BUGGER (GIBSON)

Tied by Bruce Gibson

HOOK: size 6–10 long
THREAD: Black
TAIL: Black over short red marabou with four strands of red Krystal Flash
BODY: Black chenille
HACKLE: Medium black cock, palmer style
HEAD: Black

WOOLLY BUGGER GREEN

Tied by Peter Coulson

HOOK: size 6–12 long
THREAD: Dark green
TAIL: Dark olive green marabou
UNDERBODY: Lead or copper wire (optional)
BODY: Dark green chenille
HACKLE: Large ginger cock, palmer style
HEAD: Dark green

WOOLLY BUGGER (HALL)

Tied by James Hill

HOOK: Kamasan B175, size 8–12 long
THREAD: Black
TAIL: Black marabou
BODY: Black dubbing
HACKLE: Small black cock, palmer style
EYES: Brass bead chain

This is best fished late season down and across in the Goulburn River

WOOLLY BUGGER (HILL)

HOOK: size 8–12 long
THREAD: Black
TAIL: Olive grizzle marabou
BODY: Dark olive dubbing
HACKLE: Medium black cock, palmer style
HEAD: Black tying thread

This is best fished in lakes with a slow figure-of-eight retrieve.

Tied by James Hill

WOOLLY BUGGER (HULME)

HOOK: size 6–12 long
THREAD: Black
TAIL: Black marabou with six strands of pearl tinsel
UNDERBODY: Lead or copper wire
BODY: Black chenille
HACKLE: Large black cock, palmer style
HEAD HACKLE: The fluff from large black cock hackle

This is best fished deep and slowly in rivers and lakes.

Tied by Clyde Hulme

WOOLLY BUGGER MKII

HOOK: Kamasan B830, size 8–10
THREAD: Black
TAIL: Black marabou with hot orange marabou side flashes
UNDERDODY: Lead or copper wire (optional)
BODY: Medium olive chenille
HACKLE: Natural black cock
RIB: Copper wire

The body colour may be changed to suit—olive, black, brown and even yellow has proven itself in murky water. This fly works well both weighted and unweighted.

Tied by David Dodd

WOOLLY BUGGER PURPLE (HALL)

HOOK: Wet up eye 2X long, size 8–12
THREAD: Black
TAIL: Light purple marabou with pearl Microflash
BODY: Purple chenille
RIB: Pearl tinsel
HACKLE: Large purple cock, palmer style
EYES: Lead dumbbell with 2 mm silver stick on eyes and epoxy

Tied by Mick Hall

dog tooth

SECTION TWO

NATIVE AUSTRALIAN FISH

CHAPTER 23

AUSTRALIAN BASS, BREAM & ESTUARY PERCH

BASS VAMPIRE

HOOK: Mustad 34007, size 8–1/0
THREAD: Black flat waxed
TAIL: Pearl Mylar tube small
BODY: Black Estaz chenille
WING: Black over purple Slinky Fibre
EYES: Powder-coated yellow or chartreuse dumbbell eyes

This is a top fly for bream and Australian bass. Strip the fly with 2–6 fast, short strips then a pause, then a long slow pull.

Tied by Peter Coulson

BASS VAMPIRE BLEEDING

HOOK: Mustad 34007, size 8–1/0
THREAD: Black flat waxed
TAIL: Pearl Mylar tube small
BODY: Black Estaz chenille
THROAT: Red Estaz chenille
WING: Black over purple Slinky Fibre
EYES: Powder-coated yellow or chartreuse dumbbell eyes

Fish this fly like the original Vampire. It too can be fished on all types of fly lines, floating to super fast sink.

Tied by Peter Coulson

BASS VAMPIRE CHARTREUSE

HOOK: Mustad 34007, size 8–1/0
THREAD: Chartreuse flat waxed
TAIL: Pearl Mylar tube small
BODY: Chartreuse Estaz chenille
WING: Dark olive over chartreuse Slinky Fibre
EYES: Powder-coated chartreuse dumbbell eyes

Fish this fly like the original Vampire. It too can be fished on all types of fly lines, floating to super fast sink.

Tied by Peter Coulson

BASS VAMPIRE OLIVE

HOOK: Mustad 34007, size 8–1/0
THREAD: Black flat waxed
TAIL: Pearl Mylar tube small
BODY: Olive Estaz chenille
WING: Black over olive Slinky Fibre
EYES: Powder-coated yellow dumbbell eyes

Fish this fly like the original Vampire. It too can be fished on all types of fly lines, floating to super fast sink.

Tied by Peter Coulson

Tied by Peter Coulson

BASS VAMPIRE ORANGE AND BLACK

HOOK: Mustad 34007, size 8–1/0
THREAD: Black flat waxed
TAIL: Pearl Mylar tube small
BODY: Black Estaz chenille
WING: Black over orange Slinky Fibre
EYES: Powder-coated yellow dumbbell eyes

Fish this fly like the original Vampire. It too can be fished on all types of fly lines, floating to super fast sink.

Tied by Keith Gough

BLACK & PURPLE CLOUSER

HOOK: Gamakatsu O'Shaughnessy, size 2–4
THREAD: Black flat waxed
WING: Black and purple bucktail with rainbow Krystal Flash
EYES: Painted yellow and black lead dumbbell eyes

This fly was specially developed for deep fishing in Moogerah and Maroon Dams for Australian bass. This fly can be fished fast, slow or twitched.

Tied by Peter Coulson

BREAM BUNNY BLACK

HOOK: Mustad 34007, size 8–1/0
THREAD: Black flat waxed
BODY: Black Estaz chenille
WING: Black Zonker strip
EYES: Powder coated, chartreuse dumbbell eyes
TYING NOTE: The Zonker strip is tied to the underside of the hook

Cast to structure or where fish are holding and allow the fly to sink to the required depth then strip the fly with 2–6 small and fast strips of about 30 cm then pause for 2–15 seconds, experiment until you find the most successful length of pause. While pausing you can draw the fly with a long, slow pull.

Tied by Peter Coulson

BREAM BUNNY CHARTREUSE

HOOK: Mustad 34007, size 8–1/0
THREAD: Chartreuse flat waxed
TAIL: Pearl Mylar tube small
BODY: Pearl Estaz chenille
WING: Chartreuse Zonker strip
EYES: Powder coated chartreuse dumbbell eyes
TYING NOTE: The Zonker strip is tied to the underside of the hook

Fish as Bream Bunny Black.

BREAM BUNNY PINK

HOOK: Mustad 34007, size 8–1/0
THREAD: Pink flat waxed
TAIL: Pearl Mylar Tube small
BODY: Pearl Estaz chenille
WING: Purple Zonker strip
EYES: Powder coated pink dumbbell eyes
TYING NOTE: The Zonker strip is tied to the underside of the hook

Fish as Bream Bunny Black.

Tied by Peter Coulson

BREAM VAMPIRE

HOOK: Mustad 34007, size 2
THREAD: Lime green flat waxed
TAIL: Lime green marabou
BODY: Lime green flock chenille
WING: 15 to 20 fibres of dark olive Streamer Hair
EYES: Powder coated chartreuse Brite Eyes

Fish as Bream Bunny Black.

Tied by Peter Coulson

HALO CHARLIE

HOOK: Mustad 34007 size 4
THREAD: Mono
BODY: Pearl tinsel under 10 kg mono
HALO: Chartreuse SLF
EYES: Chrome 3 mm
HEAD: Clear mono

Tied by Adam Royter

HAMMERHEAD-CHARCOAL

HOOK: Mustad Signature Tarpon C68
TAIL: BMS blend or SLF
RIB: Accent Flash
BODY: BMS blend or SLF
EYES: Dazl-Eyes

Tied by Muz Wilson

HAMMERHEAD-OLIVE

HOOK: Mustad Signature Tarpon C68
TAIL: BMS blend or SLF
RIB: Accent Flash
BODY: BMS blend or SLF
EYES: Dazl-Eyes

HAMMERHEAD-PINK

HOOK: Mustad Signature Tarpon C68
TAIL: BMS blend or SLF
RIB: Accent Flash
BODY: BMS blend or SLF
EYES: Dazl-Eyes

HAMMERHEAD-SILVER

HOOK: Mustad Signature Tarpon C68
TAIL: BMS blend or SLF
RIB: Accent Flash
BODY: BMS blend or SLF
EYES: Dazl-Eyes

JELLY BELLY VAMPIRE CHARTREUSE

HOOK: Mustad 34007, size 2
THREAD: Chartreuse flat waxed
TAIL & BODY: 5 cm chartreuse, glitter, single tail soft plastic
EYES: Powder coated, chartreuse dumbbell eyes
HEAD: Chartreuse Estaz chenille

A great fly for fishing around structure for bream and trevally and across sand flats for flathead and whiting. Allow it to sink to your chosen depth, twitch out with a short, active retrieve with pauses.

JELLY BELLY VAMPIRE PURPLE

HOOK: Mustad 34007, size 2
THREAD: Black flat waxed
TAIL & BODY: 5 cm purple, glitter, single tail soft plastic
EYES: Powder coated, chartreuse dumbbell eyes
HEAD: Black Estaz chenille

Fish as Jelly Belly Vampire Chartreuse.

Tied by Peter Coulson

JELLY BELLY VAMPIRE SILVER

HOOK: Mustad 34007, size 2
THREAD: White flat waxed
TAIL & BODY: 5 cm silver grey, single tail soft plastic
EYES: Powder coated, glow dumbbell eyes
HEAD: Pearl Estaz chenille

This variation is great for discoloured water. Fish as Jelly Belly Vampire Chartreuse.

Tied by Peter Coulson

JELLY BELLY WHITE AND PINK

HOOK: Mustad 34007, size 2
THREAD: White flat waxed
TAIL & BODY: 5 cm white and pink, single tail soft plastic
EYES: Powder coated, glow dumbbell eyes
HEAD: Pearl Estaz chenille

This variation is great for discoloured water. Fish as Jelly Belly Vampire Chartreuse.

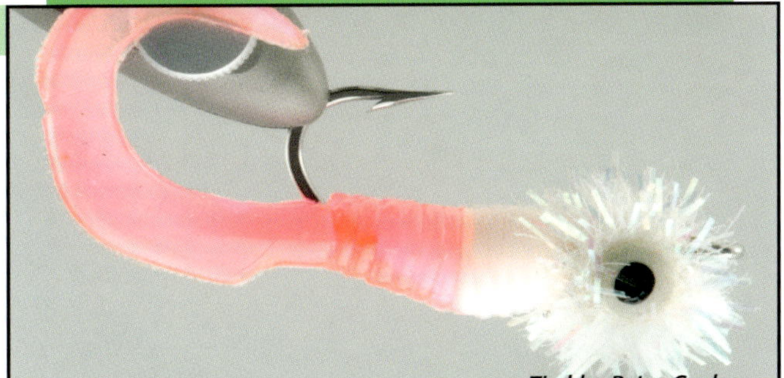
Tied by Peter Coulson

JELLY BELLY RATTLE HEAD-CHARTREUSE

HOOK: Mustad 34007, size 2
THREAD: Chartreuse
TAIL & BODY: 5 cm chartreuse, single tail soft plastic
EYES: 3 mm glass rattle eyes with 2 mm silver stick-ons
HEAD: Devcon 5 minute epoxy

This fly works best on spooky bream in clear or shallow water.

Tied by Peter Coulson

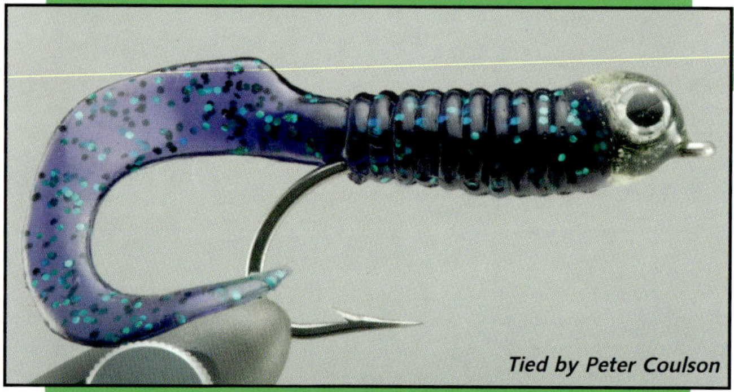
Tied by Peter Coulson

JELLY BELLY RATTLE HEAD-PURPLE

HOOK: Mustad 34007, size 2
THREAD: Black
TAIL & BODY: 5 cm Purple single tail soft plastic
EYES: 3 mm glass rattle eyes with 2 mm silver stick-ons
HEAD: Devcon 5 minute epoxy

This fly works best on spooky bream in clear or shallow water.

Tied by Peter Coulson

JELLY BELLY RATTLE HEAD-WATERMELON

HOOK: Mustad 34007, size 2
THREAD: Black
TAIL & BODY: 5 cm watermelon single tail soft plastic
EYES: 3 mm glass rattle eyes with 2 mm silver stick-ons
HEAD: Devcon 5 minute epoxy

This fly works best on spooky bream in clear or shallow water.

Tied by Keith Gough

LEZ'S LEACH MARK V

HOOK: Mustad 3666, size 4
THREAD: Black flat waxed
TAIL: Pearl Mylar tube small
BODY: Black Crystal Chenille
WING: Olive Zonker
EYES: Black bead chain

Fish this fly with 2–3 strips of 30 cm then pause for a second. This fly was developed for fishing around the weeds in Maroon Dam. I have also had success in many other dams—Hinze, Clarrie Hall and Borumba for saratoga.

Tied by Micah Adams

MICAH CHARLIE

HOOK: Mustad 34007, size 8–2/0
THREAD: Lime green flat waxed
TAIL: Lime green marabou
BODY: Lime green flock chenille
WING: 15–20 fibres of dark olive Streamer Hair
EYES: Nickel dumbbell eyes

This fly is excellent for both bream and Australian bass. Strip the fly with 3–4 small and fast pulls then pauses. Best fished on a floating or intermediate fly line.

MINI CYCLOPS

Tied By Muz Wilson

HOOK: Mustad C68 Tarpon, size 6
THREAD: Black
BODY: Chenille
OVERBODY: Green foam cylinder
CLAWS: Black rabbit
LEGS: Black saddle hackle
RIB: Copper wire

PERCH FRY

Tied by Noel Jetson

HOOK: Kamasan B200, size 4–10
THREAD: Black 8/0
BODY: Mixture of maroon and black seal's fur dubbing
TAIL: Natural squirrel tail
BODY: Pink wool in 3 sections
REAR HACKLE: Red cock
MID HACKLE: Yellow cock
FRONT HACKLE: Tan grizzle cock, swept back to form head
HEAD AND EYE: Lacquered, with yellow and black, painted eye

PROPELLER BUM

Tied By Adam Royter

HOOK: Mustad tarpon, size 2–8
THREAD: White flat waxed
TAIL: Mono with red bead burnt onto it and gold 15 mm prop
BODY: Mono
WING: Purple and red Slinky Fibre
EYES: Small painted lead dumbbell eyes
HEAD: Cover with glitter glue

THE MAY

Tied By Steve Rumney

HOOK: Kamasan B175, size 8–10
THREAD: Black
TAIL: Orange Marabou with eight strands of pearl Krystal Flash
BODY: Red wool over-wrapped with pearl Krystal Flash
LEGS: Pearl Krystal Flash
HACKLE: Red cock
HEAD: Black tying thread

This is an excellent estuary perch pattern fished at all depths and retrieves.

CHAPTER 24

FLIES FOR AUSTRALIAN NATIVE FISH

BLACK POPPER

HOOK: 3X long, size 4/0
THREAD: Black flat waxed
TAIL: Black marabou and black holographic tinsel
BODY: Black foam shaped on a drill and epoxied on to the hook shank
EYES: Silver 3D self adhesive eyes

This is best fished on hot evenings and into the night.

Tied by Peter Coulson

BLACK THING

HOOK: Mustad big gun, size 3/0
THREAD: Black flat waxed
TAIL: Black Sparkleflash
LATERAL LINE: Grizzle hackle feather one each side
UNDERWING: Krystal Flash and pearl tinsel
OVERWRAP: White Polar Fibre
OVERWING: Black Polar Fibre
COLLAR: Black rabbit
EYES: Chartreuse powder coated dumbbell
WEED GUARD: 15 kg mono, optional

Cast the fly to structure and allow it to sink to required depth. Strip the fly with 30 cm pulls and a slight pause. This pattern is excellent for cod

Tied by Peter Coulson

CHUPAFLY

HOOK: Gamakatsu, size 3/0–6/0
THREAD: Uni-Thread 1/0 or Big Fly
TAIL PIPE: Chup-a-Chup stick
BODY: Rabbit fur (Zonker strips)

This is an effective fly that works on the fish's colour-aggression factor. Professional fly tier Muz Wilson has tied some crazy 'one-offs', and this is an extension of one of them.

Tied by Adam Royter

CHUPAFLY DELUXE

HOOKS: Gamakatsu Stingers, size 2–2/0
THREAD: Uni-Thread Big Fly, white
TAIL: Flashabou, pearl
TAIL PIPE: Chup-a-Chup stick
HOOK TO HOOK CONNECTOR: 24 kg Superbraid (through stick)
RATTLE: Large Pyrex
BODY: Rabbit fur (Zonker strip)
EYES: Large lead eyes, white/black
LEGS: Rubberlegs, fluoro orange/clear with pearl fleck
OVERWING: Silver holographic Flashabou
WEED GUARD: Supa-Weld 8 kg

CHUPAFLY MEDIUM

HOOKS: Gamakatsu Stingers, size 2–2/0
THREAD: Uni-Thread Big Fly white
TAIL: Orange rabbit Zonker strip
TAIL PIPE: Chup-a-Chup stick
HOOK TO HOOK CONNECTOR: 24 kg Superbraid (through stick)
BODY: Purple and black Zonker strip

CHUPAFLY MINI

HOOK: Gamakatsu Stingers, size 1–2/0
THREAD: Uni-Thread 3/0 or Big Fly
TAIL PIPE: Cotton bud stick
BODY: Zonker strips
EYES: Large lead eye, yellow/black

This is the same as the original Chupafly only smaller. This is the fly I choose when the fish are short taking or I'm fishing in clearer water where a smaller fly is appropriate.

CYCLOPS

Tied by Muz Wilson

HOOK: TMC 8089, size 10
THREAD: Black
BODY: Chocolate brown chenille
OVERBODY: Brown foam
RIB: Copper wire
LEGS: Olive hackle
CLAWS: Brown rabbit

FOAM HEAD FURY

Tied by Adam Royter

HOOK: Eagle Claw LO67U, size 2–6/0
THREAD: Uni-Thread Big Fly
RATTLE: Wapsi fly rattles, large Pyrex
Rattle holder: Cable tie 100 x 2.5 mm black
TAIL: Whiting bronze saddles, black and hot pink
TAIL FLASH: Tiewell Reflections, purple/green
COLLAR: Marabou-purple/red
POPPER HEAD: Edgewater Boilermaker 1/0, purple
BIB: Coca-cola bottle
EYES: 3D silver
LEGS: Sililegs—black/red flake

A dirty water specialist, this fly shakes a rattle placed at 90 degrees to the hook shank because the bib makes the fly swim like a lure. Its buoyancy allows it to float off snags and be swum close to the surface for nighttime activities. A medium to slow full strip gets best results.

FURY

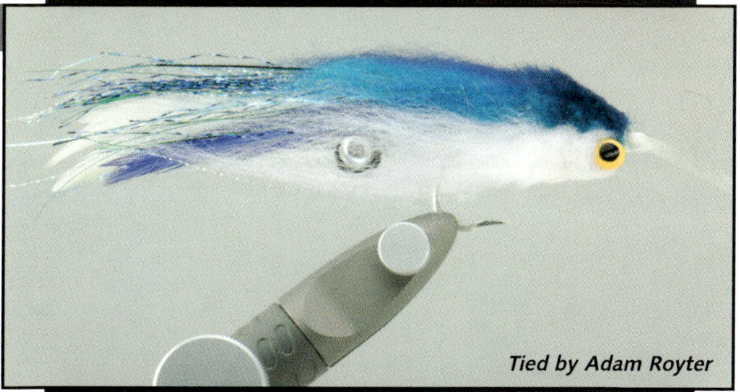
Tied by Adam Royter

HOOK: Eagle Claw LO67U, size 2–6/0
THREAD: Uni-Thread 3/0 black
RATTLE: Wapsi fly rattle, Pyrex, large
RATTLE HOLDER: Cable tie 100 x 2.5 mm, black
TAIL: Whiting bronze saddle black, pink and purple
TAIL FLASH: Flashabou blue, green and brown
BIB: Clear acetate sheet
EYES: Large lead, red/black
HEAD: Spun deer hair, black, purple and fluorescent red

The shape of the bib allows this fly to swim over snags just like a deep diving lure. It sinks quickly and has an underwater sound range of 6 metres.

Tied by Adam Royter

GOATCHEESEBOY

HOOK: Mustad 34007, size 4/0
THREAD: Black 3/0
TAIL: Pearl and glow Flashabou with some olive and black ostrich herl
COLLAR: Olive and brown marabou, black ostrich and peacock herl
HEAD: Brown deer hair, spun and clipped

This is a good fly when the goat moths are out late in the afternoon. The fly works best if it's soaked in silicon and left to dry before fishing. Best fished still or with a slow figure-of-eight retrieve.

Tied by Rob Meade

HUNTSMAN

HOOK: Gamakatsu SL12S, size 2/0–4/0
THREAD: Uni-Thread 3/0 or Big Fly red
BODY: Olive green crosscut Zonker and grizzle ostrich wrapped together
LATERAL: Pearl Krystal Flash
EYES: Large silver stick on eyes
HEAD: Red thread and epoxy

This is a great fly for Murray cod

Tied by Adam Royter

JUNGLE SPIDER

HOOK: Gamakatsu stinger, size 6
THREAD: Black 3/0
TAIL: Marabou, purple and yellow
TAIL FLASH: Black holographic Flashabou
BODY: Rainy's Round Foam, large yellow
LEGS: Round rubber, yellow
BODY COLOUR: Softex and 0.008 Holographic purple glitter
LEG COLOUR: Purple marker pen

Not tied to resemble a spider, this fly was designed to catch jungle perch and works on sooty grunter. Not so much a popper as it is a slider. This fly looks appealing even with no movement at all.

ORANGE & BLACK

HOOK: Mustad 34007, size 1/0
THREAD: Black flat waxed
TAIL: Four black cock hackles
LATERAL LINE: Grizzle hackle feather, one each side
UNDERWING: Black bucktail
OVERWRAP: Black bucktail
COLLAR: Black and orange marabou
EYES: Bead chain
HEAD: Tying thread

Cast this fly to structure and allow it to sink to required depth. Strip the fly with 300 mm pulls and a slight pause. This pattern is excellent for yellowbelly and bass.

Tied by Peter Coulson

REENEN'S REDIE

HOOK: Gamakatsu SL12S, size 2/0
THREAD: Uni-Thread, 3/0 white
BODY: Polar Fibre white, shrimp and olive
OVER FLASH: Comes Alive pearl root beer
THROAT: Fluoro Fibre 'Bleeding Gill Red'
EYES: Silver 3D eyes

The design of this fly was by Paul van Reenen from Success Flies Unfair Advantage Materials. It is a good lightweight fly with plenty of movement.

Tied by Adam Royter

ROYT'S REDFIN

HOOK: Gamakatsu Stinger, size 2
THREAD: Red 3/0
TAIL: Red marabou red and Mylar tubing, large/gold
OVERWING: Silver holographic Flashabou, silver grizzle Zonker, olive and grey fox
UNDERWING: S.L.F., white
CHIN: Red marabou
EYES: Silver 3D eyes

As it has plenty of in-built movement, this fly can be moved slowly in the snags and has a good reputation for catching big redfin and trout as well as natives.

Tied by Adam Royter

SHAGGY BLACK

Tied by Peter Coulson

HOOK: Mustad C68S SS, size 2/0
THREAD: White flat waxed
BODY: Sparkleflash black
EYES: Gold 7 mm self adhesive 3D eyes

SHAGGY DOG FROG

Tied by Peter Coulson

HOOK: Mustad C68S SS, size 2/0
THREAD: White flat waxed
BODY: Sparkleflash, yellow pearl
COLOURING: Blush pink throat and cheeks, olive green back and warm grey and black spots
EYES: Gold 7 mm self adhesive 3D eyes

SLINKY DOG

Tied by Peter Coulson

HOOK: Mustad C68S SS, size 1/0
THREAD: White flat waxed
BODY: Slinky Fibre, yellow
COLOURING: Red throat and dark brown back
EYES: Gold 7 mm self adhesive 3D eyes

SPIKE

Tied by Peter Coulson

HOOK: Mustad 2X long, size 3/0
THREAD: White flat waxed
BODY: Sparkleflash gold over yellow pearl. Tie in clumps top and bottom compressing after each clump, the thicker the better. Then trim to shape
GILLS: Red waterproof marker
EYES: Gold 7 mm self adhesive 3D eyes

WOOL HEAD FURY

Tied by Adam Royter

HOOK: LO67U 6/0–2
THREAD: Uni Thread Big Fly, white
RATTLE: Wapsi fly rattle, Pyrex, large
RATTLE HOLDER: Cable tie 100 mm x 2.5 mm black
TAIL: Whiting bronze saddle white/blue
TAIL FLASH: Tiewell Refections: blue/green, light blue Flashabou and pearl Aurora thread
BIB: Clear acetate sheet or equivalent plastic
EYES: Large yellow/black lead eyes
WOOL HEAD: Mara Wool or Polar Fibre blue/white

This is a more durable Fury for the northern freshwater and saltwater angler. With a quick change of colour you can take this fly from salt water to fresh water.

dog tooth
ATOMIC

SECTION THREE

SALTWATER

CHAPTER 25

CANDIES

BARB BIT CANDY

HOOK: Mustad 34007, size 1/0
THREAD: White flat waxed
TAIL & BODY: Streamer Hair white, chartreuse and olive green
LATERAL LINE: Chartreuse grizzle hackle tip each side
EYES: Chartreuse 3 mm self adhesive eyes
BODY: Cover whole fly excluding tail with Devcon epoxy

This is an excellent fly for Australian salmon, tailor and tuna. Retrieve this fly in long (1 m) very fast strips or with a smooth, double handed retrieve.

BOOBY CANDY LIME

HOOK: Mustad 34039NPSS, size 1
THREAD: White flat waxed
TAIL: Pearl Mylar tube
UNDERBODY: White closed cell foam
OVERBODY: Pearl E-Z body coloured lime on top with marker
EYES: Pearl 2 mm self adhesive eyes
BODY: Cover whole fly, excluding tail, with SoftDip

Fish this pattern on a full sink line on a short leader of about 0.4 m in water up to 6 m deep. Strip the fly with one or two short fast pulls, then pause. This fly can also be fished on a floating line. Retrieve to make a constant bow wave in front of the fly.

GLOW CANDY

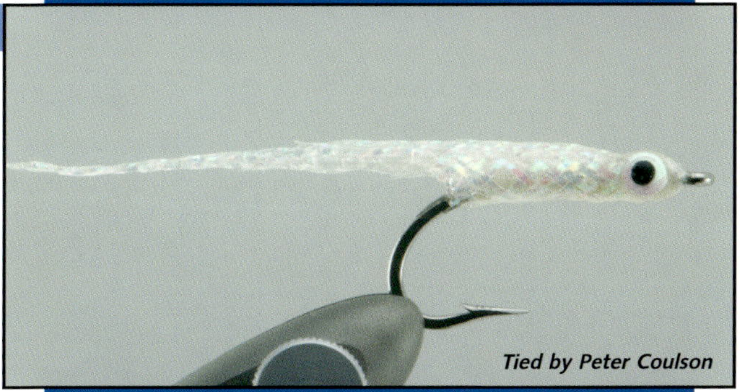

HOOK: Mustad 34007, size 4–8
THREAD: White flat waxed
TAIL: Streamer Hair, white
UNDERBODY: Glow in the dark strips
OVERBODY: Pearl Mylar tube
OVERWING: Pearl Krystal Flash, 5 fibres
EYES: Pearl self adhesive eyes
BODY: Cover whole fly, including tail, with Softex

This fly is excellent for after dark and low light estuary fishing. Strip the fly slowly with small pauses. Shine a torch or camera flash on the fly every 5–10 minutes.

Tied by Peter Coulson

GLOW EYE CANDY

HOOK: Mustad 34007, size 4–8
THREAD: White flat waxed
TAIL & UNDERBODY: Streamer Hair, dark olive over white
OVERBODY: Pearl E-Z Body tube
OVERWING: Dark green Krystal Flash 5 fibres
EYES: Glow in the dark self adhesive eyes
BODY: Cover whole fly, excluding tail, with Devcon 5 minute epoxy

This is an excellent fly for estuary and rock fishing. Strip the fly fast and slow with small pauses. This fly works well at all depths for trevally, bream, estuary perch, slimy mackerel and pike. Shine a torch on the eyes every 5–10 minutes.

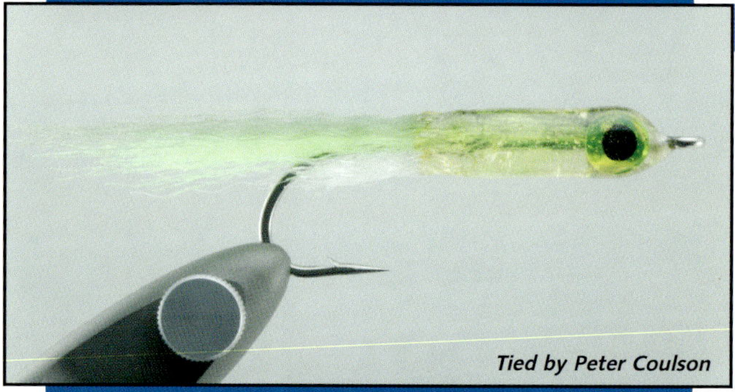

Tied by Peter Coulson

LIME CANDY

HOOK: Mustad 34039NPSS, size 1
THREAD: White flat waxed
TAIL & BODY: Streamer Hair white, chartreuse and olive green
EYES: Chartreuse 5 mm self adhesive eyes
BODY: Cover whole fly, excluding tail, with Devcon epoxy

Tied by Peter Coulson

LIME CANDY STICK

HOOK: Mustad 34007, size 1/0
THREAD: White flat waxed
TAIL & BODY: White Streamer Hair, blue pearl Sparkleflash and chartreuse Streamer Hair
EYES: Silver 5 mm self adhesive eyes
BODY: Cover whole fly, excluding tail, with Devcon epoxy

This is an excellent fly for Australian salmon, tailor, tuna and flathead. Can be retrieved in very fast half-metre strips, but a smooth, double handed retrieve, the smoother the better.

MYLAR CANDY

HOOK: Mustad 34007, size 8–5/0
THREAD: White flat waxed
TAIL: SLF Hanks in colour to suit, must be short
UNDERBODY: SLF Hanks same as tail
OVERBODY: Pearl Mylar tube
EYES: Pearl self adhesive eyes
BODY: Cover whole fly, except tail, with Devcon 5 minute epoxy

This is an excellent fly for estuary and sandflat fishing. Strip the fly fast for Australian salmon, tailor, trevally and flathead. Slow the retrieve with smaller flies for bream and estuary perch.

Tied by Peter Coulson

MYLAR CANDY 2

HOOK: Extra long shank, size 8–2/0
THREAD: White flat waxed
UNDERBODY: The cord from under Mylar tube
TAIL & OVERBODY: Pearl Mylar tube
EYES: Pearl self adhesive eyes
BODY: Cover whole fly, except tail, with Devcon 5 minute epoxy

This is an excellent fly for estuary and sandflat fishing. Strip the fly fast for Australian salmon, tailor, trevally and flathead. Slow the retrieve with smaller flies for bream and estuary perch.

Tied by Peter Coulson

SKEETER UV PEARL

HOOK: Mustad C68S SS, size 6
THREAD: White flat waxed
BODY: Sparkleflash UV pearl, tied shaggy dog style
EYES: Silver 2 mm self adhesive eyes
OVERBODY: Cover whole fly with 2 coats of SoftDip

This fly sits in the surface film and leaves a small bow wave with each 10 cm strip. Pause every fifth or sixth strip. Most strikes will occur on the pause.

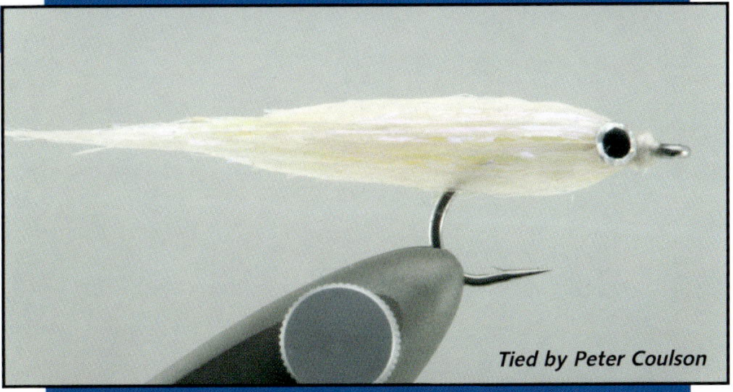

Tied by Peter Coulson

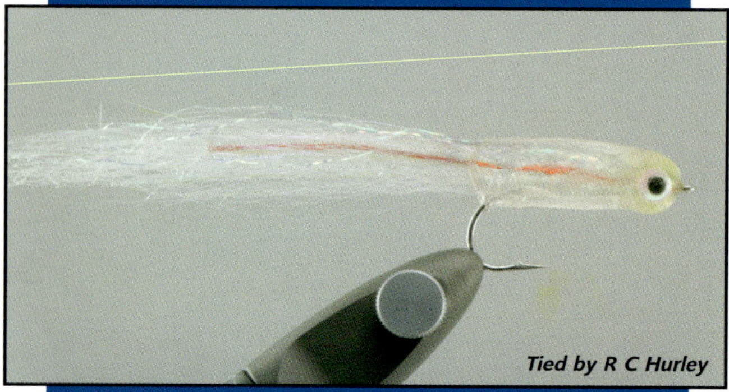

RC CANDY

HOOK: Mustad S71S SS, size 4
THREAD: White flat waxed
UNDERBODY: Pearl tinsel
TAIL & BODY: Light bright grey, 4 strands of Sparkleflash, 4 strands of red flat waxed thread-Softex together with translucent Slinky Fibre
OVERBODY: Clear silicone
HEAD: Five minute epoxy
EYES: Pearl 5 mm self adhesive eyes

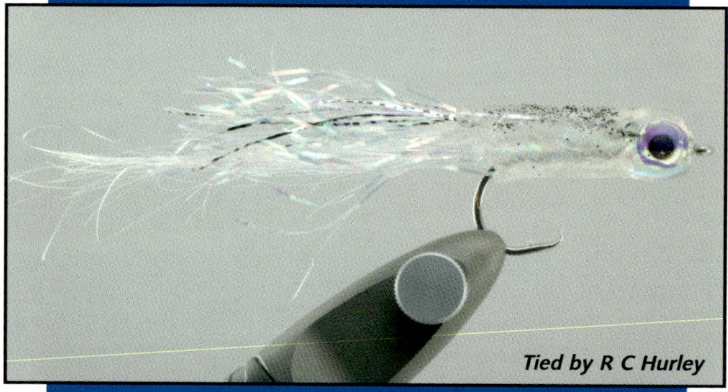

RC CANDY SALT 'N' PEPPER

HOOK: Mustad C71S SS, size 4
THREAD: White flat waxed
TAIL & BODY: Light bright grey, Mylar motion pearl blue teased out, Unique hair, Shimmerflash and translucent Slinky Fibre
OVERBODY: Pearl E-Z body covered with clear silicone and superfine black glitter
HEAD: Five minute epoxy
EYES: Pearl blue Mirage eyes

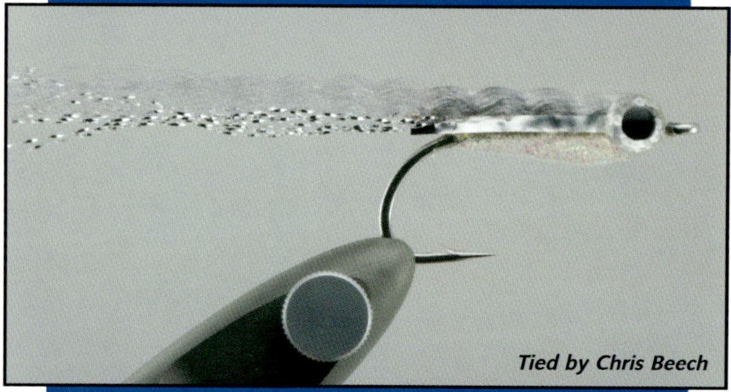

SOFTEX SURF SARDINE

HOOK: Mustad 34044, Tiemco 811S, Black Magic Salt Water Fly, size 1–2/0
THREAD: White flat waxed nylon
BODY: Silver Sparkle Braid or Maxi Braid
WING: Several strands of silver Krystal Flash topped with grey Ultra Hair
LATERAL LINE: Wide silver Mylar
EYES: Silver 3.5 mm 3-D Prism eyes
BELLY: Pearl E-Z Shape Sparkle Body
FINISH: Coat entire body of fly with three coats of Softex

A chewy morsel that rarely fouls on the cast!

SLIMY CANDY

HOOK: Extra long shank, size 3/0–5/0
THREAD: White flat waxed
UNDERBODY & TAIL: White bucktail and olive green Streamer hair
BODY: Medium pearl E-Z Body
OVERBODY: Dark olive Krystal Flash tied in at the head then laid over the E-Z Body and coated with Devcon 5 minute epoxy
HEAD: Form a cone shaped head with tying thread
EYES: Silver pearl 5 mm self adhesive eyes
FINISHING: Put some black dots on the back with a marker and cover whole fly, except tail, with Devcon 5 minute epoxy

This fly works well on schools of slimy mackerel. Fish a fast sinking line into the school and double hand strip very fast in the same direction the mackerel are swimming.

Tied by Lionel Coombs

SURF CANDY BLUE BACK

HOOK: Mustad 34007, size 4–4/0
THREAD: White Danville's flat waxed nylon
BODY: Super Hair or Streamer Hair with a few strands of Krystal Flash, blue on purple on sky blue on white
EYES: Prism Tape eyes
RED GILLS: Nail polish or model paint

Experiment with various speeds of retrieve. Trim the tail of the fly to suit.

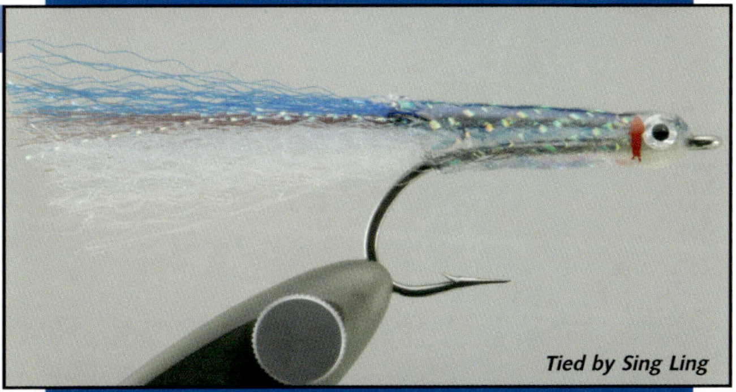

Tied by Sing Ling

SURF CANDY CHARTREUSE

HOOK: Mustad 34007, size 4–4/0
THREAD: White Danville's flat waxed nylon
BODY: Super Hair or Streamer Hair with a few strands of Krystal Flash, purple on green on chartreuse on white
EYES: Prism Tape eyes
RED GILLS: Nail polish or model paint

Experiment with various speeds of retrieve. Trim the tail of the fly to suit.

Tied by Sing Ling

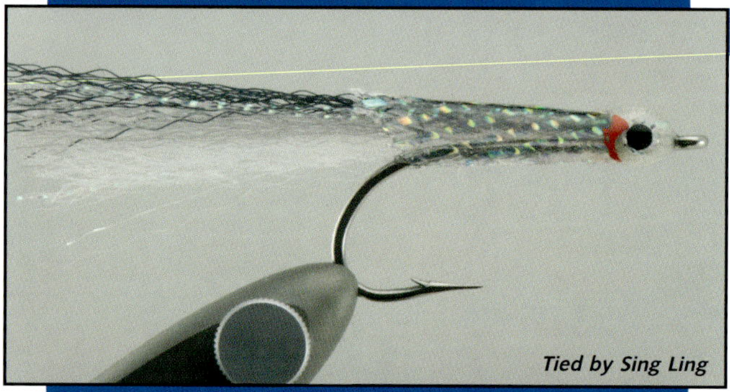

Tied by Sing Ling

SURF CANDY DARK BACK

HOOK: Mustad 34007, size 4–4/0
THREAD: White Danville's flat waxed nylon
BODY: Super Hair or Streamer Hair with a few strands of Krystal Flash, dark blue on grey on white
EYES: PrismTape eyes
RED GILLS: Nail polish or model paint

Experiment with various speeds of retrieve. Trim the tail of the fly to suit.

Tied by Chris Beech

SURF CANDY-OLIVE

HOOK: Mustad 34044, Tiemco 811S, Black Magic Salt Water Fly, size 1–2/0
THREAD: White flat waxed nylon
BODY: Silver Sparkle Braid or Maxi Braid
COLLAR: Smoke Ultra Hair topped with four strands each of silver and pearl Krystal Flash
TOPPING: Olive Ultra Hair, between which is two strands of UV grey Krystal Flash
EYES: Silver 3.5 mm self adhesive eyes
FINISH: Two coats of 5 minute epoxy, from hook eye to bend, sprinkle opal Crystal Glitter on belly after first coat.

Tied by Peter Coulson

WHITEBAIT CANDY

HOOK: Mustad 34007, size 1/0
THREAD: White flat waxed
TAIL & BODY: Streamer Hair white, silver Sparkleflash and olive green Streamer Hair
EYES: Silver 2 mm self adhesive eyes
BODY: Cover whole fly, excluding tail, with Devcon epoxy

This is an excellent fly for Australian salmon, tailor and flathead. Can be retrieved in very fast half-metre strips, but a very smooth double-handed retrieve is better.

WHITEBAIT CANDY MINI

HOOK: Mustad 34007, size 2
THREAD: White flat waxed
TAIL & BODY: Streamer Hair white, silver Sparkleflash and Streamer Hair olive green
EYES: Silver 2 mm self adhesive eyes
BODY: Cover whole fly, excluding tail, with Devcon epoxy

This is an excellent fly for Australian salmon, tailor and trevally.

Tied by Peter Coulson

WHITEBAIT CANDY PELAGIC

HOOK: Tiemco SP600, size 1/0
THREAD: White flat waxed
TAIL & BODY: Streamer Hair white, silver Sparkleflash and Streamer Hair olive green
EYES: Silver 3 mm self adhesive eyes
BODY: Cover whole fly, excluding tail, with Devcon epoxy

This pattern was developed to catch large pelagic fish feeding on small baitfish.

Tied by Peter Coulson

CHAPTER 26

CHARLIES & CLOUSERS

BAY ANCHOVY CLOUSER DEEP MINNOW

Tied by Chris Beech

HOOK: Mustad 34044, Tiemco 811S, Black Magic Salt Water Fly, size 1–2/0
THREAD: White flat waxed nylon
EYES: Chrome Dazzle Eyes or Hour Glass Eyes or Brite Eyes, black painted pupil
WING: White bucktail, four strands each of pearl, silver and UV grey Krystal Flash, silver Sparkleflash, Mylar Motions or Polar Flash, olive bucktail topped with dark olive bucktail

This pattern is a close approximation of local bay anchovies.

BEECAM NIPPER

Tied by Chris Beech

HOOK: Mustad 34044, Tiemco 811S, Black Magic Salt Water Fly, size 1–2/0
THREAD: Fluoro pink flat waxed nylon
EYES: Spirit River I-Balz, gold or black
TAIL: Light gold Tiewell Fly Fur
BODY: Pearl Mylar over which is Clear V-Rib, with a hot orange band of thread behind eyes
WING: Light gold Tiewell Fly Fur over which is four strands of root beer Krystal Flash

Designed to imitate a saltwater yabby or nipper.

CHARTREUSE CLOUSER

Tied by Peter Coulson

HOOK: Mustad 34007, size 4–2/0
THREAD: Chartreuse flat waxed
UNDERWING: Translucent white bucktail, only 10 fibres, and 4 strands of gold holographic tinsel
OVERWING: Chartreuse bucktail
EYES: Nickel coated dumbbell eyes

This is one of the best all-round patterns for the Northern Territory and Queensland.

CHARTREUSE CLOUSER BENDBACK

HOOK: Mustad 34007, size 4–2/0, bent
THREAD: Chartreuse flat waxed
UNDERWING: Translucent white bucktail only 10 fibres and 4 strands of gold holographic tinsel
OVERWING: Chartreuse bucktail
EYES: Nickel coated dumbbell eyes

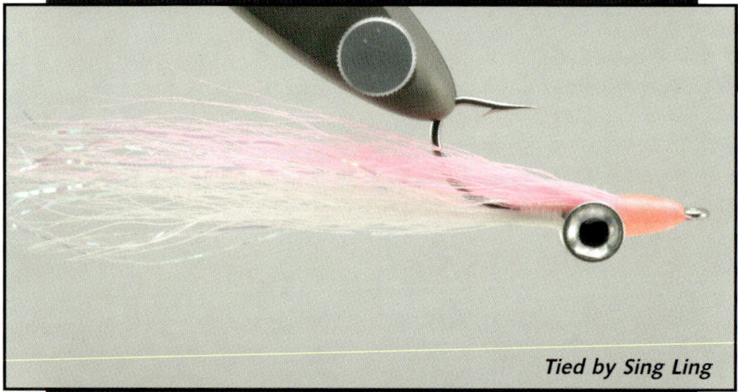

Tied by Sing Ling

CLOUSER MINNOW WITH DEEP SEA EYES

HOOK: Mustad 34007, S71SSS, size 4–2/0
THREAD: Danville's flat waxed nylon, colour to suit
UNDERWING: White calf tail or bucktail
MIDDLEWING: 4–6 strands of Krystal Flash or Sparkleflash
OVERWING: Various colours of calf tail or bucktail
EYES: Deep Sea eyes with 3D self adhesive eyes
HEAD: A layer of epoxy for extra durability

This is best fished with short strips followed by a pause; experiment with various speeds of retrieve.

Tied by Peter Coulson

GLOW IN DARK VAMPIRE GREE

HOOK: Mustad 34007, size 2
THREAD: Chartreuse flat waxed
BODY: Glow in the Dark Chenille yellow
WING: Sparkleflash Glow in the Dark green pearl
EYES: Powder coated glow in dark medium Brite Eyes

Shine a torch or camera flash on the fly. When the fly reaches the requir depth strip the fly with 2–6 small and fast strips of about 30 cm then pause for 2–15 seconds; experiment to find the most successful timing. can draw the fly with a long slow pull. This fly also works well on dark, overcast days.

GLOW IN DARK VAMPIRE PINK

Tied by Peter Coulson

HOOK: Mustad 34007, size 2
THREAD: Pink flat waxed
BODY: Glow in the Dark Chenille pink
WING: Sparkleflash Glow in the Dark pink pearl
EYES: Powder coated glow in dark medium Brite Eyes

Shine a torch or camera flash on the fly. When the fly reaches the required depth strip the fly with 2–6 small and fast strips of about 30 cm then pause for 2–15 seconds; experiment to find the most successful timing. You can draw the fly with a long slow pull. This fly also works well on dark, overcast days.

GREEN SHRIMP CHARLIE

Tied by Adam Royter

HOOK: Gamakatsu SS15, size 8
THREAD: Tan 3/0
BODY: Pearl Crystal Chenille
OVERWING: Kinky Fibre, live shrimp and saddle hackle tips, chartreuse
EYES: Bead chain, large

This is a good tropical flats fly, works well on trevally, flathead, mullet, bream, dart etc.

HALO CHARLIE TAN

Tied by Adam Royter

HOOK: Mustad 34007, size 4
THREAD: Monofilament
BODY: Pearl tinsel under 10 kg monofilament
HALO: Tan SLF
EYES: Chrome 3 mm
HEAD: Clear monofilament

Tied by Adam Royter

HALO CHARLIE WHITE

HOOK: Mustad 34007, size 4
THREAD: Monofilament
BODY: Pearl tinsel under 10 kg monofilament
HALO: White SLF
EYES: Chrome 3 mm
HEAD: Clear monofilament

Tied by Chris Ellemor

HOPPER BOMB

HOOK: TMC 800S, size 10–4/0
THREAD: Orange flat waxed
TAIL: Orange bucktail and yellow Krystal Flash
BODY: Orange Super Salt Chenille
EYES: Painted dumbbell eyes, to suit size of hook

Tied by Adam Royter

HOT CHILLI CHARLIE

HOOK: Gamakatsu SS15, size 8
THREAD: White 3/0
BODY: Pearl Crystal Chenille
OVERWING: Pearl Flashabou and fluorescent red rabbit fur
EYES: Bead chain, large

This fly is a classic all-rounder. It will catch fish anywhere.

JELLY TAIL CHARLIE

HOOK: Mustad 34007, size 2–4
THREAD: Flat waxed to suit body colour
TAIL & BODY: Sparkle pink, single tail soft plastic
WING: Pink calf tail
TOPPING: Pink Krystal Flash
EYES: Silver bead chain

Tied by Terry Hayden

MARABOU TAILED DEEP CLOUSER

HOOK: Mustad 34007, size 2/0–4/0
THREAD: White flat waxed
TAIL: Red marabou
BODY: Silver tinsel
WING: White bucktail and blue Krystal Flash
EYES: Silver bead chain eyes

Tied by Terry Hayden

MINI CHARLIE

HOOK: Mustad 8260D, size 10
THREAD: Uni 6/0 Tan
BODY: Uni-Flex-Fuchsia
OVERWING: Marabou white/pink
EYES: Bead chain small

A good fly for poking around the rocks in search of reef fish. It can be cast on a 4 weight which makes most fish feel like good ones. Retrieve in small sharp strips.

Tied by Adam Royter

Tied by Matt Wales

RATTLING MATT

HOOK: Mustad 34007, size 2
THREAD: Blue flat waxed
STOPPER: Tying thread and epoxy
BODY: Pearl and blue glass beads
WING: White and blue bucktail with Krystal Flash mixed in
EYES: Real Eyes with silver self adhesive eyes
HEAD: Blue flat waxed coated with epoxy

This is a great fly for fishing around sandflats in dirty water.

Tied by Peter Coulson

SLINKY FIBRE CLOUSER BLUE

HOOK: Mustad 34007, size 4–2/0
THREAD: Blue flat waxed
UNDERWING: Translucent white Slinky Fibre and 4 strands of silver Gliss 'N' Glow
OVERWING: Blue Slinky Fibre
EYES: Powder coated blue dumbbell eyes with yellow pupils

Retrieve this fly with long very fast strips of about a metre or with 2–6 small and fast strips of about 30 cm then pause 2–15 seconds; experiment to find the most successful timing. You can draw the fly with a long slow pull.

Tied by Peter Coulson

SLINKY FIBRE CLOUSER CHARTREUSE

HOOK: Mustad 34007, size 4–2/0
THREAD: Chartreuse flat waxed
UNDERWING: Translucent white Slinky Fibre and 4 strands of silver Gliss 'N' Glow
OVERWING: Chartreuse Slinky Fibre
EYES: Powder coated chartreuse dumbbell eyes

Retrieve this fly with long very fast strips of about a metre or with 2–6 small and fast strips of about 30 cm then pause 2–15 seconds; experiment to find the most successful timing. You can draw the fly with a long slow pull.

SLINKY FIBRE CLOUSER PINK

HOOK: Mustad 34007, size 4–2/0
THREAD: Pink flat waxed
UNDERWING: Translucent white Slinky Fibre and 4 strands of pearl Krystal Flash
OVERWING: Pink Slinky Fibre
EYES: Powder coated pink dumbbell eyes

Retrieve this fly with long very fast strips of about a metre or with 2–6 small and fast strips of about 30 cm then pause 2–15 seconds; experiment to find the most successful timing. You can draw the fly with a long slow pull.

Tied by Peter Coulson

TRAILBLAZER

HOOK: Mustad 34044, Tiemco 811S, Black Magic Salt Water Fly, size 1–2/0
THREAD: Fluoro pink flat waxed nylon
CONE: Spirit River Hot Cone
EYES: Medium chrome bead chain
BODY: Pearl Mylar
WING: Tan rabbit fur tuft

Tied as a whiting fly, it is also effective drifted in a berley trail.

Tied by Chris Beech

CHAPTER 27

CRUSTACEA

AGRO SHRIMP

Tied by Sing Ling

HOOK: Mustad 34007, size 4–2/0
THREAD: Danville's flat waxed nylon shell pink
FORELEGS: Tan HIVIS
MOUTH: Orange yarn
ANTENNAE: Two strands of shell pink Krystal Flash
EYES: Burnt 20 kg mono painted black
BODY: Crystal Chenille
LEGS: Palmered natural or dyed grizzle hackle
SHELLBACK: Pearl Krystal Flash topped with white Super Hair or Streamer Hair extended past eye of hook to form tail
WEED GUARD: 10–15 kg mono bent into inverted 'V'
WEIGHT: Chrome barbell eyes
OVERCOAT: Clear epoxy

This fly is best fished on the flats with sinking line. Cast the fly out and let it sink to the bottom. The weed guard and the weight will make the fly 'stand up' on the bottom. Retrieve it with short strips followed by a pause to create a puff of sand attracting nearby fish's attention.

AGRO SHRIMP GREEN

Tied by Sing Ling

HOOK: Mustad 34007, size 4–2/0
THREAD: Danville's flat waxed nylon shell pink
FORELEGS: Tan HIVIS
MOUTH: Orange yarn
ANTENNAE: Two strands of olive Krystal Flash
EYES: Burnt 20 kg mono painted black
BODY: Green Crystal Chenille
LEGS: Palmered natural or dyed grizzly hackle
SHELLBACK: Pearl Krystal Flash topped with white Super Hair or Streamer Hair extended past eye of hook to form tail
WEED GUARD: 10–15 kg mono bent into inverted 'V'
WEIGHT: Brass barbell eyes
OVERCOAT: Clear epoxy

This fly is best fished on the flats with sinking line. Cast the fly out and let it sink to the bottom. The weed guard and the weight will make the fly 'stand up' on the bottom. Retrieve it with short strips followed by a pause to create a puff of sand attracting nearby fish's attention.

BACKSIDE CRAB

Tied by Adam Royter

HOOK: Mustad 34007, size 1/0
THREAD: Uni Big Fly, white
LEGS: Turkey feather, knotted
SHELL: Deer skin
EYES: Burnt 20 kg mono
EYES UNDERBODY: Lead plain, XL
UNDERBODY: Lambs wool

Effective on many different fish species including flathead, mulloway, salmon and bream. This imitation is of a feeding crab and can be moved slowly across a sandy bottom with a figure-of-eight retrieve.

Tied by Peter Coulson

BAITED BREATH

HOOK: Mustad 34007, size 2–4
THREAD: Danville's flat waxed nylon shell red
ANTENNAE: Two stripped grizzle hackle quills
MOUTH & LEGS: Grizzle hen hackle
EYES: Burnt 20 kg mono painted black
BODY: Grey dubbing mix
BACK: Clear Shell Back
RIB: Copper wire
TAIL TAG: Red thread

Tied by Peter Coulson

CLEAR WATER SHRIMP

HOOK: Mustad 34007, size 4
THREAD: White flat waxed
UNDERBODY: Sparkleflash chenille UV pearl
BODY: Slinky Fibre, white
ANTENNA: Pearl Krystal Flash
EYES: Black mono eyes
FINISH: Two coats of clear epoxy on the back and head with a sprinkle of fine black glitter between coats

This fly is excellent for both bream and Australian bass. Cast the fly to fish or structure then strip the fly with 3–4 short and fast pulls, then pause. It is best fished on a floating or intermediate line.

Tied by Lionel Coombs

COOMBS MUSSEL

HOOK: Mustad 34007, size 8
THREAD: White flat waxed
GILLS: Translucent white Streamer Hair
BODY: Black cardboard
OVERBODY: Clear epoxy

Cast the fly to fish or structure, then fish dead drift. It is best fished on a floating or intermediate line.

CORAL CRAB

HOOK: Mustad 34007, size 2
THREAD: White flat waxed
LEGS: Four well-marked pheasant breast feathers
BODY: Cream cardboard covered in Mrs Simpson feathers and epoxy
EYES: Black mono eyes

Cast to fish on sandflats or structure where fish are holding and allow the fly to sink. Retrieve this fly with 1–3 small and fast strips of about 10 cm then pause for 2–15 seconds; experiment to find the most successful timing. You can draw the fly with a long slow pull.

Tied by Peter Coulson

CRAWLING CRAB

HOOK: Mustad 34007, size 2
WEIGHT: Lead wire, optional
LEGS & CLAWS: Knotted braided monofilament
BODY: Hook and loop fasteners, cut into disks and glued together
EYES: Black and yellow Joggle Eyes

If fishing to sighted fish, often the best retrieve is to simply do nothing. Let the fish find it, and maybe twitch it slightly if fish swim past.

Tied by Max Garth

HAYNES CLEAR SHRIMP

HOOK: Mustad 34007, size 4
THREAD: White flat waxed
UNDERBODY: Translucent white streamer hair
ANTENNA & OVERBODY: Pearl Krystal Flash
EYES: Black mono eyes
FINISH: Two coats of clear epoxy and black dots with waterproof marker between coats

This fly is excellent for both barramundi and mangrove jacks. Cast the fly to fish or structure then strip the fly with 3–4 short and fast pulls then pause. Best fished on a floating or intermediate line.

Tied by Peter Haynes

Tied by Peter Haynes

HAYNES SHRIMP

HOOK: Mustad 34007, size 2/0
THREAD: White flat waxed
TAIL: Tan and white bucktail with a bunch of pearl Krystal Flash in the middle
BODY: Soft white cock tied palmer style and clipped on the top and sides
OVERBODY: Pink crystal fabric paint
EYES: Black monofilament eyes

This fly is excellent for far north Australian estuary fishing. Cast the fly to fish or structure then strip the fly with short and fast 30 cm pulls. It is best fished on a floating or intermediate line.

Tied by Terry Hayden

MODIFIED BAITED BREATH

HOOK: Mustad 34007, sizes 6–1/0
THREAD: White flat waxed
TAIL: White rabbit fur and pearl Krystal Flash
BODY: White chenille or wool
HACKLE: White saddle hackle, palmered
EYES: White plastic beads, connected on mono

Tied by Adam Royter

MUD SHRIMP

HOOK: Mustad 34007, size 5/0
THREAD: White flat waxed
FEELERS: Krystal Flash and fox tail
MOUTH: Olive marabou and pearl tinsel
NIPPERS: Grizzle hackle stripped to shape nippers.
BODY & LEGS: Olive rabbit
EYES: 20 kg mono burnt
RIB: Mono cord
BACK: Partridge feather coated with Soft Dip
TAIL: Olive marabou

ONE ARMED BANDIT

HOOK: 4X long, size 4
THREAD: White 3/0
FEELERS: pearl Aurora thread and Polar Fibre white, shrimp and pink
EYES: Burnt 40 kg mono
CLAWS: Polar Fibre white, shrimp and pink and Softex
LEGS AND BODY: Polar Fibre white, shrimp and pink
SHELL: Felt and Softex
RIBBING: White Uni-Flex

Tidal estuary systems with large expanses of sand and mud flats are the places where you will find the bass yabby, and fish this fly.

Tied by Adam Royter

PINKBACK SHRIMP

HOOK: Mustad 34007, size 4–2/0
THREAD: White flat waxed
MOUTH: Brown micro fibre
EYES: Burnt 20 kg mono, painted black
BODY: Pearl tinsel
LEGS: Palmered natural or dyed grizzle hackle
ANTENNAE, SHELLBACK & TAIL: Pink Streamer Hair extended past eye of hook to form tail
OVERCOAT: Clear epoxy

Tied by Peter Coulson

RC FLATS FLY

HOOK: Mustad 34007, size 2
THREAD: Black flat waxed
EYES: Chrome dumbbell eyes
BODY: Create a frame using mono tied from the front of the eyes and tied off at the bend. Coat with 5 minute epoxy and black glitter to form body
WING: Black bucktail, red Krystal Flash and a pair of black hackle tips

Tied by R C Hurley

Tied by R C Hurley

RC 4C

HOOK: Mustad 34007, size 2
THREAD: Tan flat waxed
EYES: Gold dumbbell eyes
BODY: Create a frame using mono tied from the front of the eyes and tied off at the bend. Coat with 5 minute epoxy and gold glitter to form body
TAIL: Natural bucktail
WING: Natural bucktail and gold Krystal Flash

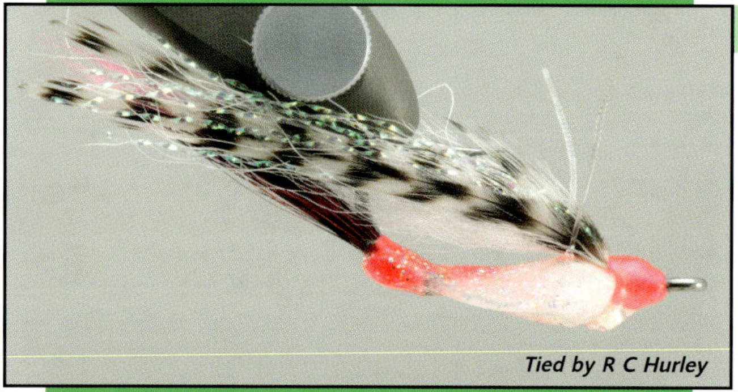

Tied by R C Hurley

RC 4C PINK SHRIMP

HOOK: Mustad 34007, size 2
THREAD: Hot pink flat waxed
UNDER BODY: Hot pink flat waxed
TAIL: Hot pink bucktail
EYES: Chrome dumbbell eyes
BODY: Create a frame using mono tied from the front of the eyes and tied off at the bend. Coat with 5 minute epoxy and pearl glitter to form body
WING: White bucktail, pearl Krystal Flash and a pair of grizzle hackle tips
WEED GUARD: Monofilament
HEAD: Hot pink

Tied by R C Hurley

RC SHRIMP

HOOK: Mustad 34007, size 5/0
THREAD: White flat waxed
FEELERS: Pearl Krystal Flash, ShimmerFlash, yellow and white Lite Brite
BODY: Pearl chenille Estaz chenille
LEGS: Large grizzle cock
RATTLE: Pyrex large inside E-Z body
RIB: 10 kg stainless wire
TAIL: Pearl Krystal Flash
SHELLBACK: Five minute epoxy
EYES: 20 kg mono, burnt
WEIGHT: Chrome dumbbell eyes

RC 4C SHRIMP BLACK

HOOK: Mustad 34007, size 2
THREAD: Black flat waxed
EYES: Chrome dumbbell eyes
BODY: Create a frame using mono tied from the front of the eyes and tied off at the bend. Coat with 5 minute epoxy and black glitter to form body
WING: Black bucktail, red Krystal Flash and a pair of black hackle tips

Tied by R C Hurley

ROCK CRAB (HAYNES)

HOOK: Mustad 34007, size 2
THREAD: Black flat waxed
TAIL & LEGS: Three black hackle tips
BODY: Black Velcro covered in Devcon epoxy
EYES: Black mono eyes
MOUTH: Red nail polish

Cast to fish on sandflats or structure where fish are holding and allow the fly to sink. Retrieve this fly with 1–3 small and fast strips of about 10 cm then pause for 2–15 seconds; experiment to find the most successful timing. You can draw the fly with a long slow pull.

Tied by Peter Haynes

ROCK CRAB (COOMBS)

HOOK: Mustad 34007, size 2
THREAD: Black flat waxed
LEGS: 4 black Mrs Simpson feathers
BODY: Black cardboard covered in black Mrs Simpson feathers and epoxy
EYES: Black mono eyes
MOUTH: Red nail polish

Cast to fish on sandflats or structure where fish are holding and allow the fly to sink. Retrieve this fly with 1–3 small and fast strips of about 10 cm then pause for 2–15 seconds; experiment to find the most successful timing. You can draw the fly with a long slow pull.

Tied by Peter Coulson

SAND CRAB

HOOK: Mustad 34007 size 2
THREAD: White flat waxed
LEGS: 4 cream pheasant breast feathers
BODY: Cream cardboard covered in cream pheasant breast feathers with the odd tan markings and epoxy
EYES: Black mono eyes

Cast to fish on sandflats or structure where fish are holding and allow the fly to sink. Retrieve this fly with 1–3 small and fast strips of about 10 cm then pause for 2–15 seconds; experiment to find the most successful timing. You can draw the fly with a long slow pull.

TAN SHRIMP

HOOK: Mustad 34007, size 2–4
THREAD: Flat waxed black
ANTENNAE: Two Krystal Flash fibres
MOUTH & LEGS: Grizzle brown hen hackle tips and tan calf tail
EYES: Burnt 20 kg mono painted black
BODY: Tan chenille
RIB: Black wire
HACKLE: Grizzle hen swept back
TAIL TAG: Black thread

TIGER PRAWN

HOOK: Mustad 34007, size 5/0
THREAD: Uni Big Fly, white
FEELERS: Mullet brown Kinky Fibre and pearl Aurora thread
LEGS: Polar Fibre, white
EYES: 20 kg mono
RATTLE: Pyrex large
BODY: Pearl chenille large
SHELL TOP: Polar Fibre shrimp over olive
RIB: Uni Flex camel

A medium to large sized prawn pattern that performs well. Fast 30 cm retrieves with a pause will get the best out of the rattle inside the fly.

WALES SHRIMP

Tied by Matt Wales

HOOK: Mustad 34007, size 5/0
THREAD: White flat waxed
FEELERS: Stripped grizzle quills
MOUTH: White rabbit guard hairs
NIPPERS: Grizzle hackle stripped to shape nippers. The quill is threaded inside Gudebrod and barbed with a waterproof marker.
BODY: Pearl Estaz chenille
LEGS: Large grizzle cock
EYES: 20 kg mono burnt
RIB: Mono coloured with waterproof marker
BACK & TAIL: Pearl green Krystal Flash
SHELLBACK: Five minute epoxy marked with a waterproof marker
WEED GuARD: 27 kg stainless wire (optional)

ULTRA SHRIMP

Tied by Paul Williamson

HOOK: Mustad 34007, size 8–2/0
THREAD: Flat waxed nylon
ANTENNA: Black Krystal Flash
TAIL: Light brown or tan Neer Hair with a flash of orange
BODY: Tan, dun or grey synthetic dubbing
LEGS: Grizzle hackle, palmered
EYES: 15 kg mono burnt and painted black
SHELLBACK: Streamer Hair, epoxy with Devcon

Fish the unweighted version with little twitches or at dead drift.

ULTRA SHRIMP 11

Tied by Paul Williamson

HOOK: Mustad 34007, size 8–2/0
THREAD: Flat waxed nylon
ANTENNA: Black Krystal Flash
TAIL: Light brown or tan Neer Hair with a flash of orange
BODY: Tan, dun or grey synthetic dubbing
LEGS: Grizzle hackle, palmered
EYES: 15 kg mono burnt and painted black
SHELLBACK: Streamer hair, epoxy with Devcon
WEIGHT: Small dumbbell eyes
SUPPORTS: 7 kg mono

Tied with the weight and supports, the shrimp will adopt a defensive pose.

CHAPTER 28

POPPERS

BIG BOY POPPER

HOOK: Mustad 34007, size 6/0
THREAD: White flat waxed
UNDERTAIL: Sparkleflash silver pear
OVERTAIL: Teased out silver E-Z body
BODY: White closed cell corking foam covered with E-Z body and dipped in SoftDip
EYES: Silver 10 mm self adhesive eyes

Tied by Peter Coulson

BALSAWOOD POPPER

HOOK: 3X long, size 3/0
THREAD: White flat waxed
TAIL: White bucktail, holographic tinsel and white/pink marabou
BODY: Balsawood shaped with a dermal tool and painted red and white
EYES: 5 mm eyes

Tied by Peter Coulson

CHUGGER

HOOK: 3X long, size 4/0
THREAD: White flat waxed
TAIL: Sparkleflash silver pearl spun and clipped
BODY: White closed cell corking foam hollowed out at the front and coated with SoftDip and silver glitter
HEAD: Red nail polish
EYES: Silver 7 mm self adhesive eyes cut top and bottom

This fly is great for giant trevally and queenfish.

Tied by Peter Coulson

CORKER

HOOK: Mustad 34007, size 3/0
THREAD: White flat waxed
TAIL: Four white and two grizzle saddle hackles and 8 strands of Gliss 'N' Glow
BUM: Grizzle marabou
BODY: White closed cell corking foam coated with SoftDip and silver glitter
EYES: Silver 3D eyes

Tied by Peter Coulson

CORKER GREEN

HOOK: Mustad 34007, size 3/0
THREAD: White flat waxed
TAIL: Four green grizzle saddle hackles
BUM: Green grizzle marabou
BODY: White closed cell corking foam coated with green SoftDip
LEGS: Rubber legs, braided
EYES: Red 3D eyes

FIZZER

HOOK: 3X long, size 2/0
THREAD: White flat waxed
TAIL: White bucktail, holographic tinsel and white/pink marabou
BODY: Foam thong shaped with a dermal tool
BLADE: Perspex corrugated sheet cut to shape
EYES: Red and white paint

FROGGER

HOOK: 3X long, size 1/0–2/0
THREAD: White flat waxed
TAIL: Rubber skirt from a spinnerbait
LEGS: Rubber skirt from a spinnerbait
BODY: White closed cell corking foam coloured with waterproof marker and covered in 2 coats of SoftDip

LEE'S GURGLER

HOOK: Mustad 34007, size 2/0–1
THREAD: Pink flat waxed
UNDERTAIL: Sparkleflash silver
OVERTAIL: White bucktail
BODY: Large pearl Krystal Flash
OVERBODY: Yellow Evazote
THROAT: Red Krystal Flash

This pattern was designed as an easy-to-cast alternative to the conventional popper. It is excellent for barramundi in shallow water when retrieved with short sharp strips. It is also great for saratoga, trevally, queenfish and mangrove jack around snags and effective in dams for bass.

MINI POPPER

HOOK: Mustad 34007, size 1
THREAD: White flat waxed
TAIL: Four grizzle saddle hackles
HACKLE: Grizzle
BODY: White EVA foam shaped with a dermal tool
EYES: Gold 5 mm 3D eyes

Tied by Peter Coulson

MYLAR POPPER

HOOK: 3X long, size 2/0
THREAD: Red flat waxed
TAIL: Yellow and white marabou
BODY: White EVA foam shaped with a dermal tool and covered with yellow pearl Mylar and epoxy
EYES: Gold 7 mm eyes

Tied by Peter Coulson

POPPER BLACK

HOOK: 2X long, size 1/0
THREAD: Black flat waxed
TAIL: Black marabou and holographic tinsel
BODY: Black EVA foam shaped with a dermal tool
EYES: Silver 5 mm 3D eyes

This is a good fly for around mangroves and structure late afternoon and night.

Tied by Peter Coulson

POPPER GREEN

HOOK: 3X long, size 1/0
THREAD: White flat waxed
TAIL: Green and black marabou
LEGS: Green and black rubber skirt from a spinnerbait
BODY: Green EVA foam shaped with a dermal tool
EYES: 5 mm 3D eyes
WEED GUARD: 27 kg wire

This is a good fly for around mangroves and structure.

Tied by Peter Coulson

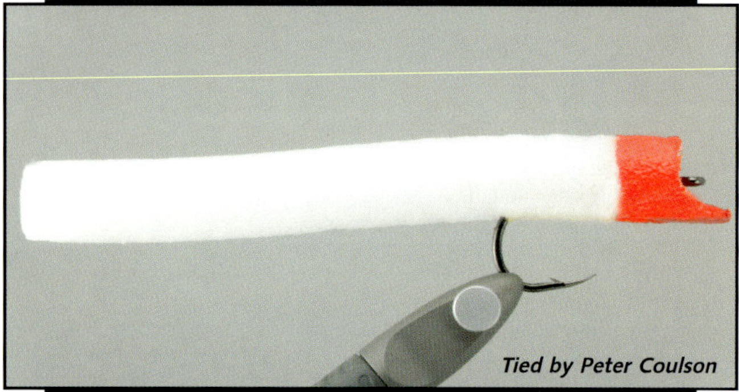

Tied by Peter Coulson

POP STICK

HOOK: Mustad big gun, size 2/0
THREAD: White flat waxed
BODY: White closed cell corking foam coated in SoftDip
HEAD: Red nail polish

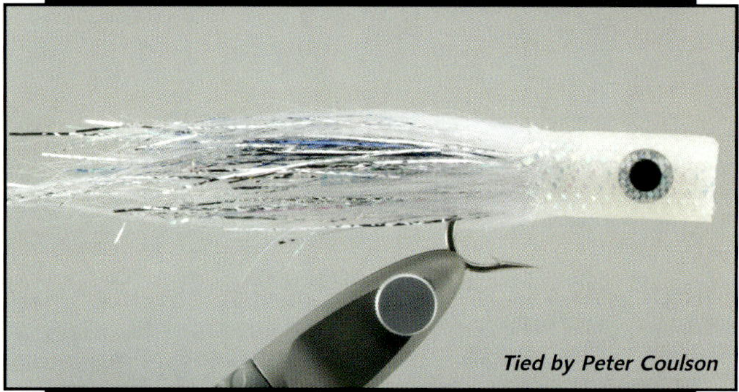

Tied by Peter Coulson

REACTOR

HOOK: Mustad 34007, size 1/0
THREAD: White flat waxed
UNDERTAIL: Sparkleflash silver
OVERTAIL: White Polar Fibre lightly covering the whole tail
BODY: White closed cell corking foam covered with E-Z body and dipped in SoftDip
EYES: Silver 7 mm self adhesive eyes

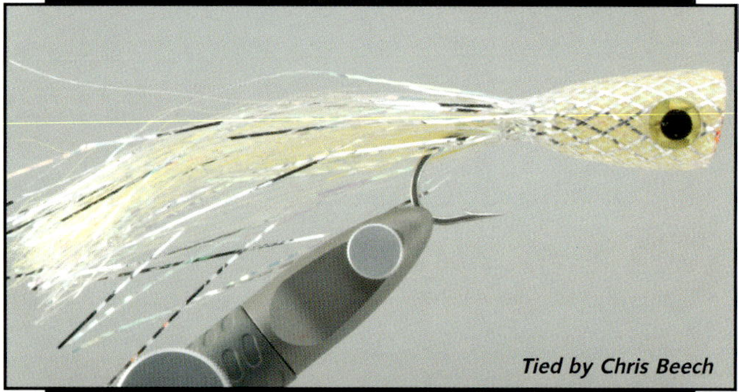

Tied by Chris Beech

SOFT POPPER

Hook: Mustad 34039, 33903, Tiemco 511S, size 1/0–4/0
Tail: Kinky Fibre or Ultra Hair (for a more buoyant fly, bucktail)
Body: Edgewater popper body (boilermaker or pencil popper)
Braid: Light Wapsi Flexi-Cord, fixed to foam body with Softex
Eyes: 3.5 mm self adhesive eyes, fixed with Softex

A soft, squishy popper that is easy to tie.

Tied by Allan Barber

SOFT POPS

HOOK: Tiemco 8089, size 1/0–4/0
TAIL: Fine chartreuse Rubberlegs with purple and gold Gliss 'N' Glow
BODY: Soft Pops yellow bottom and purple top, glued to the hook and shaped with a sharp knife
OVERBODY: Pearl sheet and Devcon epoxy
EYES: 7 mm 3D eyes

SOFT POPS FROG

HOOK: Tiemco 8089, size 2–2/0
LEGS: Grey and black fine Rubberlegs
BODY: Soft Pops cream glued to the hook and shaped with a sharp knife
OVERBODY: Pearl sheet and Devcon epoxy
EYES: 7 mm 3D eyes

Tied by Allan Barber

STINGER

HOOKS: Mustad 34007, size 2/0
THREAD: White flat waxed
TAIL: Sparkleflash UV silver
BODY: White closed cell corking foam covered in SoftDip
EYES: Silver self adhesive eyes 7 mm

This pattern is great for tailor and other species that chop at the tails.

Tied by Peter Coulson

STUMPY

HOOK: Long shank, size 2
TAIL: 4–6 blue saddle hackles
COLLAR: Red saddle hackle
BODY: Flexi-Cord
EYES: Holographic self adhesive eyes, fixed with epoxy

This is a snag-resistant popper due to the shape of the face.

Tied by Terry Hayden

WHITE AND RED POPPER

HOOK: 3X long, size 1/0
THREAD: White flat waxed
TAIL: White bucktail, silver Krystal Flash and white/pink marabou
BODY: White EVA foam shaped with a dermal tool
EYES: Pearl 5 mm 3D eyes
HEAD: Red nail polish

Tied by Peter Coulson

CHAPTER 29

GENERAL SALTWATER FLIES

ANSWER TO SOFT PLASTIC

HOOK: Gamakatsu SS15T, size 2
THREAD: White flat waxed
TAIL: Estaz chartreuse SoftDip, flattened at the end
BODY: Estaz root beer and gold
HACKLE: Soft dark brown grizzle hackle
HEAD: 7 mm gold cone over hot red bead

This fly is best fished with an erratic retrieve for most estuary species.

Tied by Robert Hurley

BABY GAR

HOOK: Gamakatsu SS15T, size 8
THREAD: 6/0 white
TAIL: Pearl grizzle hackles and Aurora thread
BODY: Polar Fibre, white and grey
EYES: Silver 3D eyes
BEAK: Uni-Flex, red

This is a quality fly for fishing bays and estuary systems where juvenile garfish spend their first few months. It is a consistent catcher of species such as salmon, tailor, flathead, barracouta etc.

Tied by Adam Royter

BARRA DECEIVER

HOOK: Mustad 34007, size 2/0–6/0
THREAD: Pink flat waxed
TAIL: 6–10 white hackle feathers
UNDERBODY: Silver gift wrap or Mylar
LATERAL LINE: Barred saddle hackle feathers
OVERBODY: White bucktail and pearl Flashabou with pink bucktail on top
CHEEKS: Fluoro pink Polar Fibre

For barramundi the fly is best worked with a medium speed, long strip then pause action. The rod should always be pointed at the fly as it is retrieved. When striking, pull on the fly line before raising the rod.

Tied by Dave Donald

Tied by Adam Royter

BEC'S FRY

HOOK: Tiemco 811, size 1/0
THREAD: Uni Thread 3/0
TAIL: Supreme Hair, clear and blue holographic fibre
COLLAR & HEAD: Lambs wool, white
EYES: Silver 3D eyes
MARKER PENS: Light blue/dark blue

I love this fly. It's quick to tie, stands up to all sorts of punishment, holds its shape well in the water, is a dream to cast and most of all looks like a baitfish. This pattern was inspired by my partner Bec who is always coming up with nifty ideas.

Tied by Adam Royter

BEC'S FRY M1

HOOK: Mustad 34007, size 2/0
THREAD: 3/0 white
TAIL: Supreme Hair, clear
TAIL FLASH: Pearl Aurora thread
BODY: Tiewell Mara Wool, white and red for throat
EYES: 3D pearl
MARKER PENS: Olive/black

The M1 is designed to be fished in both fresh and salt water. With its very light colouring it will represent an amazing array of baitfish. As this fly holds its fish-like shape so well, you can let it dead drift like a stunned bait.

Tied by Peter Coulson

BIG EYE

HOOK: Mustad 34007, size 8–4/0
THREAD: White or red
TAIL: Pearl Mylar tube, teased out
UNDERBODY: Pearl Mylar tube
OVERBODY: 5 kg stainless steel trace wire
EYES: Pearl self adhesive eyes
BODY: Cover whole fly, except tail, with Devcon 5 minute epoxy

This is an excellent fly for New South Wales estuary fishing. Strip the fly at medium to fast speeds for Australian salmon, tailor and flathead. This fly works well at all depths.

BLACK & BARRED

Tied by Sing Ling

HOOK: Mustad 34007 or Gamakatsu SL12S, size 2–6/0
THREAD: Red or hot pink Danville's flat waxed nylon
TAIL: Black bucktail, pearl Pearlescent flash, 4–6 black neck hackles with 1 or 2 grizzle neck hackles tied to each side
WING: Black bucktail with a few strands of holographic Mylar Motion tied around the tail (glow in the dark Mylar Motion is optional)
COLLAR: Black marabou but Zonker strip or similar is generally more durable
EYES: Black or silver Deep Sea eyes with 3D self adhesive eyes
HEAD: Black Chenille

This fly is best fished with short strips followed by a pause, however do experiment with various speeds of retrieve.

BOOF'S BLUE FIN

Tied by Adam Royter

HOOK: Mustad 34007, size 1
THREAD: Uni Big Fly, white
BODY: Polar Fibre, white, shrimp, olive and grey
BODY FLASH: Pearl Flashabou
THROAT: Red Comes Alive
EYES: Silver 3D eyes

A typical baitfish pattern. The blending of the four colours of Polar Fibre makes the fly's back colouration suit a wide range of baitfish.

DARK GREEN SHAD-BIBBED

Tied by Adam Royter

HOOK: Eagle Claw L067U, size 1/0
THREAD: Uni Big Fly, white
BELLY: Kinky Fibre, live shrimp
MIDDLE BODY: Supreme Hair, dark green
TOPPINGS: Black holographic Flashabou
THROAT: Fluro Fibre, gill red
EYES: Pearl 3D eyes
BIB: Clear acetate sheet
MARKER PENS: Black, green and red
GLITTER: Lavender holographic 0.008
HOOK BEND LEAD: Four turns of 0.030

DR. WORM

Tied by Adam Royter

HOOKS: Mustad 8260D, tail size 10, head size 8
THREAD: Uni 6/0, tan
TAIL & BODY: Marabou, light brown/red
HEAD: Marabou, light brown/red dubbing
EYES: Plain lead, small
HOOK CONNECTION: 15 kg Super braid

This is good for sandflat fishing on species such as whiting, mullet, trevally, flathead etc. A slow figure-of-eight retrieve gets the best out of this fly.

EVERSWIM MINNOW

Tied by Adam Royter

HOOK: Gamakatsu SL12S, size 2
THREAD: 3/0 white
TAIL: Cock hackle: white
TAIL FLASH: Aurora Thread, pearl and black holographic Flashabou
BODY: Mylar tubing, holographic silver medium
EYES: Silver self adhesive eyes
BIB: Clear flexible plastic
BODY COLOUR: Softex and 0.008 holographic purple glitter

This fly is at its best in moving water. It is designed to be fished in an estuary system where the tidal movement creates flow. This fly can swim in the current without having to retrieve line. The bib allows the fly to swim like a minnow. The shape of the bib also makes the fly dive and hold in the water at high speeds.

FLATHEAD BENDBACK

Tied by Chris Beech

HOOK: Mustad 34044-bent or Tiemco 411S size 2–1/0
THREAD: Chartreuse flat waxed nylon
TAIL: Red hackle barbs
BODY: Pearl Mylar wrapped with clear V-Rib, glue before wrapping body
WING: White bucktail, several strands of multi-mix Krystal Flash then chartreuse bucktail
CHEEKS: Natural grizzle saddle, same length as the wing

This is tied as a shrimp imitation for shallow water; it is very effective on flathead. It can be weighted with lead wire wrapped under the body materials.

FULL BODY

HOOK: 34007, size 1/0
THREAD: 3/0 black
TAIL & BODY: Black marabou and medium pearl Flexi-Cord
HEAD: Masterbright, peacock green
EYES: Silver 3D eyes

Tied to imitate a small baitfish, this fly is able to be chewed by toothy fish and still be fishable. It is a hardy fly that works like a charm.

Tied by Adam Royter

GOLDBOMBER RATTLER

HOOK: Mustad keel hook, size 3/0
THREAD: White flat waxed
BODY: Sparkleflash holographic gold, with a little black in the back
RATTLE: 20 mm glass rattle tied to the bottom of the keel
EYES: Hot red 7 mm 3D self adhesive eyes

This fly fishes best in northern Australia.

Tied by Peter Coulson

HOT HEAD

HOOK: Gamakatsu SL12S, size 2/0
THREAD: Uni Big Fly, white
TAIL: Supreme Hair, white, grey and green
HEAD: Marabou, dubbed red
EYES: Silver 3D eyes

This is a good fly for high speed pelagics. This fly is designed to be able to be cut down to size if need be. An oversized hook allows for the fly to wedge itself under the jaw bone of small tuna species. The overall weight of this fly is low, allowing it to be cast on light outfits. The preferred retrieve is as fast as you can go!

Tied by Adam Royter

Tied by Chris Beech

JIGGY HABIT

HOOK: Gamakatsu Big Game, Mustad Signature Big Game
THREAD: White flat waxed nylon
BEAD: 7 mm Brite Bead
WING: Pearl Mylar Motions or Sparkleflash followed by white bucktail, tied short. Longer white bucktail on top, followed by several strands of pearl Krystal Flash, followed by longest bunch of white bucktail. Top with several strands of silver Mylar Motions, Sparkleflash or Polarflash, then olive bucktail with a few strands of UV grey Krystal Flash between.
TOPPING: Peacock Herl
EYES: Silver 3.5 mm self adhesive eyes, added after first coat of epoxy is applied over thread wraps.
HEAD: Epoxy over

This fly is designed to get down deep, fast! It is particularly effective when schools are busting up on the surface—this fly will sink quickly to where the bigger fish are lurking.

Tied by Keith Gough

KG BOMBER

HOOK: Mustad 34007, size 4/0
THREAD: Black flat waxed
TAIL: Two black and two grizzle saddle hackle feathers
UNDERWING: Orange bucktail
WING: Black bucktail
LATERAL LINE: Gold Krystal Flash and gold Gliss 'N' Glow
EYES: Black on red 7 mm self adhesive eyes
HEAD: Z-Poxy

This is an excellent fly for estuary cod, barramundi and mangrove jack in the Northern Territory, Nerang and Tweed rivers. This fly is best fished with a short, sharp strip.

Tied by Keith Gough

KG REDHEAD

HOOK: Mustad 34007, size 4/0
THREAD: Orange flat waxed
TAIL: Four white saddle hackle feathers
WING: White bucktail and silver Krystal Flash
COLLAR: Red rabbit
EYES: Silver 5 mm self adhesive eyes
HEAD: Z-Poxy

This is an excellent fly for queenfish, trevally and Spanish mackerel in the Northern Territory and the Kimberley. It also works well in the Southport Seaway for trevally and tailor. I prefer to strip this fly with a medium to fast retrieve.

KILLER CALAMARI

Tied by Adam Royter

Cone Section
TUBE: Fisker Design, 3 inch
THREAD: Uni Big Fly white
CONE: White Supreme Hair and pearl Flashabou
UNDER CONE: Crystal Chenille, pearl and white marabou

Head Section
HOOK: Gamakatsu Octopus, size 7/0
THREAD: Uni Big Fly, white
LEGS: Pearl CFC Juicy Legs, white saddle hackle and pearl Flashabou
HEAD: Home made eyes 15 mm, silver and black, red and white Cactus chenille and white and fluoro pink Polar Fibre

Squid are a popular food source for many game fish. This pattern is tied with lightweight materials for easy casting and has a large enough hook to get a good hold on any fish. This fly can be stripped fast or left on a dead drop.

MAKO DOG

Tied by Peter Coulson

HOOK: Mustad C68S SS, size 6/0
STINGER: Mustad C68S SS, size 4/0
THREAD: White flat waxed
BODY: Sparkleflash belly shine
LATERAL LINE: Large pearl lateral line
COLOURING: Red head
EYES: Silver 7 mm 3D self adhesive eyes

This is my all-time favourite Mako shark fly. I only cast this fly to sighted sharks. I don't blind flog this pattern.

MARABOU MUD THING

Tied by Adam Royter

HOOK: Mustad 34044, Tiemco 811S, size
TAIL: Purple gold and blue Reflections or Krystal Flash surrounding glass rattle, with one yellow grizzle saddle hackle on each side
COLLAR: Dyed yellow squirrel tail and olive grizzly marabou
EYES: Brass bead chain
HEAD: Yellow/black variegated chenille

MARABOU SQUID

Tied by Peter Coulson

HOOK: Mustad 34007 size 1/0
THREAD: Pink flat waxed
TAIL: Pink and black marabou
BODY: Peach chenille
COLLAR: Pink marabou
EYES: Pearl 7 mm 3D eyes

This is an excellent fly for blue throat wrasse, trevally and Australian salmon. I like to strip this fly with a medium to fast, jerky retrieve.

MEGA DOG

Tied by Peter Coulson

HOOK: Mustad C68S SS, size 6/0
STINGER: Mustad C68S SS, size 4/0
THREAD: White flat waxed
BODY: Sparkleflash UV pearl and Shimmerflash micro silver
LATERAL LINE: Silver Slinky fibre
COLOURING: Red, green, purple and indigo blue
EYES: Silver 7 mm 3D self adhesive eyes

This is a great offshore pattern.

MUD THING

Tied by Chris Beech

HOOK: Mustad 34044, Tiemco 811S, size
TAIL: Gold Sparkleflash or Polarflash surrounding glass rattle
COLLAR: Dark yellow bucktail outside of which is a dyed yellow grizzle saddle each side
HACKLE: Two dyed yellow grizzle and one dyed olive grizzle saddle
EYES: Gold I-Balz or Round End eyes
HEAD: Yellow/black or yellow/brown speckled chenille or Variegated Chenille

This fly was commissioned by Scott Mitchell to look like a Gold Bomber lure.

PARTS & PIECES SHARK FLY

Tied by Adam Royter

HOOKS: Gamakatsu, size 8/0 x 2
THREAD: Uni Big Fly black
HOOK WIRE: 135 lb nylon-coated 7 strand, plus crimps
TAIL AND BODY: Gill red Comes Alive and purple, tan and red marabou

Sharks of all species will have a swipe at this fly. Thrown in front of a worked-up shark in the berley trail and given an occasional 'twitch', this fly is a work of art.

PINK THING (Haynes)

Tied by Peter Haynes

HOOK: Mustad 34007, size 1/0
THREAD: White flat waxed
TAIL: White Streamer hair
LATERAL LINE: Grizzle hackle feather, one each side
UNDERWING: Krystal Flash and pearl tinsel
OVERWRAP: White bucktail
OVERWING: Purple bucktail
COLLAR: Pink soft hackle
EYES: Yellow dumbbell
WEED GUARD: 15 kg mono, optional
HEAD: Tying thread coated with glitter fabric paint

Cast the fly to structure and allow it to sink to the required depth. Strip the fly with 30 cm pulls and a slight pause. This pattern is excellent for barramundi, mangrove jacks and giant trevally.

PINK EYE

Tied by Adam Royter

HOOK: Gamakatsu SL12S, size 2/0
THREAD: Uni Big Fly white
TAIL: Polar Fibre, white and pink
TAIL FLASH: Pearl Aurora thread and holographic silver Flashabou
SIDE HACKLES: Whiting bronze saddle, hot pink
COLOUR: Hot pink marabou
EYES: Pearl 3D eyes
Marker pen: Black

Following in the footsteps of the mighty Pink Thing, the Pink Eye is another variation on a great tropical saltwater fly.

Tied by Peter Coulson

PILCHARD HEAD

HOOK: Tiemco TMC 600SP, size 1/0–4/0
THREAD: White flat waxed
BUTT: Large clump of red and black Slinky Fibre tied in above hook point and trimmed off at the bend
UNDERWING: White Slinky Fibre
OVERWRAP: Sparkleflash silver
OVERWING: Grey Slinky Fibre
EYES: Yellow 7 mm self adhesive eyes
FINISHING: Colour the fly to suit with waterproof markers then coat it with three coats of SoftDip

Form a berley trail using cubes or pilchards cut to about the same size as the fly; be sure not to over berley. Feed one cube about every ten seconds. Once your berley trail has formed, cast the fly into the trail and allow it to dead drift down the berley trail. After about three minutes strip the fly back quickly then re-cast. Most fish take the fly on dead drift but some fish will hit the fly hard on the retrieve.

Tied by Adam Royter

POLAR FIBRE MINNOW

HOOK: Mustad big gun, size 2
THREAD: Uni 3/0 white
BODY: White and black Polarflash
LATERAL LINE: Slinky Fibre, silver
THROAT: FluoroFibre, bleeding gill red
MARKINGS: Black waterproof marker
EYES: Silver self adhesive
HEAD: 5 minute epoxy

The design of this fly was by Paul van Reenen from Success Flies Unfair Advantage Materials, the rest was left up to us. It is a good lightweight fly with plenty of movement.

Tied by Peter Coulson

POLARSPARKLE WHITEBAIT

HOOK: Mustad Big Gun size 2–1/0
THREAD: White flat waxed
UNDERBODY: Sparkleflash dark olive pearl over silver
LATERAL LINE: Gliss 'N' Glow, 4 fibres each side
OVERBODY: White Polar Fibre lightly covering the whole fly
EYES: Silver 3D self adhesive eyes
HEAD: Devcon 5 minute epoxy

This is an excellent fly for pelagic and predator fishing. Strip the fly fast to very fast for mackerel, tuna, bonito, Australian salmon, and tailor. The fly works well when cast to the outer edges of a feeding school and retrieved with long sharp pulls.

POLARSPARKLE BLUEBAIT

Tied by Peter Coulson

HOOK: Mustad Big Gun, size 2–1/0
THREAD: White flat waxed
UNDERBODY: Sparkleflash dark blue rainbow and emerald rainbow over silver
LATERAL LINE: Gliss 'N' Glow 4 fibres and one blue grizzle hackle tip each side
OVERBODY: White Polar Fibre lightly covering the whole fly and blue on top
EYES: 3D self adhesive eyes
HEAD: Devcon 5 minute epoxy

This is an excellent fly for pelagic and predator fishing. Strip the fly fast to very fast for mackerel, tuna, bonito, Australian salmon and tailor. The fly works well when cast to the outer edges of a feeding school and retrieved with long sharp pulls.

POLARSPARKLE YELLOWBAIT

Tied by Peter Coulson

HOOK: Mustad Big Gun, size 2–1/0
THREAD: White flat waxed
UNDERBODY: Sparkleflash yellow pearl over silver
LATERAL LINE: Gliss 'N' Glow 4 fibres each side
OVERBODY: White Polar Fibre lightly covering the whole fly, and chartreuse on top
EYES: Chartreuse 3D self adhesive eyes
HEAD: Devcon 5 minute epoxy

This is an excellent fly for pelagic and predator fishing. Strip the fly fast to very fast for mackerel, tuna, bonito, Australian salmon and tailor. The fly works well when cast to the outer edges of a feeding school and retrieved with long sharp pulls.

POLARSPARKLE MULLET

Tied by Peter Coulson

HOOK: Mustad Big Gun, size 2–1/0
THREAD: White flat waxed
UNDERBODY: Sparkleflash holographic lime over silver
OVERBODY: White Polar Fibre lightly covering the whole fly and mark dark olive green stripes with waterproof marker
EYES: Silver 3D self adhesive eyes
HEAD: Devcon 5 minute epoxy

This is an excellent fly for pelagic and predator fishing. Strip the fly fast to very fast for mackerel, tuna, bonito, Australian salmon and tailor. The fly works well when cast to the outer edges of a feeding school and retrieved with long sharp pulls.

Tied by Adam Royter

POLY

HOOK: Long shank 6
THREAD: 1 kg monofilament
TAIL: Orange marabou
UNDER BODY: 2 layers of 0.35 lead
OVER BODY: Red chenille

The Poly is an excellent fly for parrotfish and also good on other small to medium southern reef fish. Although not the most durable, it is quick to tie and very expendable. It is best fished with a berley trail.

Tied by R. C. Hurley

POP LIP GREEN

HOOK: Mustad, size 2–3/0
THREAD: White flat waxed
TAIL: Four lime green under four dark green saddle hackle feathers with lime Krystal Flash over
BODY & BIB: Green/grey Mara Wool spun and trimmed to shape, Bob Popovic style
OVERBODY: Clear silicone
EYES: Green self adhesive eyes

Tied by R. C. Hurley

POP LIP ORANGE

HOOK: Mustad, size 2–3/0
THREAD: White flat waxed
TAIL: Four lime green under four orange saddle hackle feathers with pearl Sparkleflash over
BODY & BIB: Yellow/orange Mara Wool spun and trimmed to shape, Bob Popovic style
OVERBODY: Clear silicone
EYES: Silver self adhesive eyes

POP LIP PINK

HOOK: Mustad, size 3/0–2
THREAD: White flat waxed
TAIL: Six white and two dark grizzle saddle hackle feathers with pearl Krystal Flash over
BODY & BIB: Pink Mara Wool spun and trimmed to shape, Bob Popovic style
OVERBODY: Clear silicone
EYES: Red self adhesive eyes

Tied by R C Hurley

PUPPY DOG GHOST

HOOK: Mustad C68S SS, size 2
THREAD: White flat waxed
BODY: Sparkleflash translucent pearl and Slinky fibre pearl
COLOURING: Red gills with grey insides with waterproof marker
EYES: 4 mm 3D self adhesive eyes

Tied by Peter Coulson

PUPPY DOG NITRO

HOOK: Mustad C68S SS, size 2
THREAD: White flat waxed
BODY: Sparkleflash silver and UV pearl
COLOURING: Sunburst yellow crimson red
EYES: Gold 4 mm 3D self adhesive eyes

A great variation for estuaries.

Tied by Peter Coulson

Tied by Peter Coulson

PUPPY DOG SPOT

HOOK: Mustad C68S SS, size 2
THREAD: White flat waxed
BODY: Sparkleflash UV pearl
COLOURING: Bronze and black back, bronze and black spot
EYES: Pearl Glow in the Dark 4 mm 3D self adhesive eyes

This pattern fishes well around mangroves and structure with a short jerky strip. Best fished on floating or intermediate lines.

Tied by Peter Coulson

PUPPY DOG SUNSET

HOOK: Mustad C68S SS, size 2
THREAD: White flat waxed
BODY: Yellow pearl Sparkleflash
COLOURING: Orange with red head and spots, with black back and stripes
EYES: Pearl gold 3 mm 3D self adhesive eyes

A great variation for estuaries.

Tied by Peter Coulson

PUPPY DOG WHITEBAIT

HOOK: Mustad C68S SS, size 2
THREAD: White flat waxed
BODY: UV pearl Sparkleflash
COLOURING: Cool grey, warm grey, dark green on top
EYES: Silver 4 mm 3D self adhesive eyes

This is one of those patterns that just work everywhere, on any fish with any retrieve. I have caught more than 50 species on this pattern from barramundi to snapper, kingfish to bream.

RC'S AUSSIE RED HEAD SCAD

TUBE: Fisker Design, 3 inch
THREAD: Uni Big Fly red
BODY: Streamer Hair white, shrimp, light blue, lime and chartreuse
BODY FLASH: Fine pearl Shimmerflash
LATERAL LINE: Large pearl Shimmerflash
GILLS: Black waterproof marker
BLEEDING HEAD: Red bucktail
EYES: Silver 10 mm 3D eyes
HEAD: Red thread

RC'S SLIMY MACKEREL

TUBE: Fisker Design, 3 inch
THREAD: Uni Big Fly white
BODY: Streamer Hair translucent white, grey and light blue
BODY FLASH: Fine pearl blue and pearl Shimmerflash
LATERAL LINE: Large pearl and silver holographic Shimmerflash
MARKINGS: Black waterproof marker
HEAD: Thread
EYES: Pearl 10 mm 3D eyes

RC'S GOLD BOMBER

HOOK: Gamakatsu, size 6/0
THREAD: Gold
UNDERBODY: White Streamer Hair
OVERBODY: Holographic gold Shimmerflash and gold Sparkleflash
MARKINGS: Red and black waterproof marker for gills and throat
EYES: Silver 3D self adhesive eyes large
HEAD: Softex

Tied by R C Hurley

RC'S PINK SQUID

HOOK: Mustad 34007,size 2–1/0
THREAD: White flat waxed
TAIL: Six white saddle hackle feathers marked with a pink waterproof marker, pink Krystal Flash and grizzle Shimmerflash
FINS: Form a frame with 10 kg mono and cover with Softex and pearl glitter
OVERBODY: Softex and pearl glitter
EYES: Silver 3D self adhesive eyes

Tied by R C Hurley

RC'S SQUID

HOOK: Mustad 34007, size 2–1/0
THREAD: White flat waxed
TAIL: Six white saddle hackle feathers, pearl Sparkleflash and grizzle Shimmerflash
FINS: Form a frame with 10 kg mono and cover with Softex and pearl glitter
OVERBODY: Softex and pearl glitter
EYES: Silver 3D self adhesive eyes

Tied by Adam Royter

ROYT'S BIG FISH TUBE FLY

TUBE: Fisker Design, 3 inch
THREAD: Uni Big Fly, white
BODY: Success Flies Kinky Fibre, fluorescent white, live shrimp, belly shine and chartreuse
BODY FLASH: Pearl Flashabou
UNDERBODY: Large silver holographic Mylar tube
BLEEDING HEAD: Root bear and gill red Comes Alive
EYES: Home made 15 mm gold and black eyes

This fly can be used successfully on all large predatory fish with no exceptions. Being a tube fly, it can be quickly changed and has the ability to slide up the line when a fish is jumping. This reduces the overall leverage on the hooks.

SAND SPRAT

Tied by Adam Royter

HOOK: Mustad 34044, Tiemco 811S, Black Magic Salt Water Fly, size 1–2/0
THREAD: White flat waxed nylon
BODY: Pearl Sparkleflash Braid or Maxibraid
COLLAR: Polar Bear EP Fibres (or HIVIS, Neer Hair)
TOPPING: Four strands each of pearl and silver Krystal Flash then grey EP fibres
CHEEKS: 4–5 strands of silver Sparkleflash, Mylar Motions or Polarflash
Eyes: Silver 3.5 mm 3D Prism Eyes, epoxy between eyes

This is tied as an imitation of the sand sprat—an important forage fish in southern waters.

SHAGGY DOG BLUE BARB

Tied by Peter Coulson

HOOK: Mustad C68S SS, size 2/0
THREAD: White flat waxed
BODY: Sparkleflash UV pearl
COLOURING: Chartreuse belly, crimson red throat, blush pink cheeks, peacock green back and barb
EYES: Gold 7 mm 3D self adhesive eyes

The colouring of this fly was based on a popular lure. This fly fishes best in northern Australia.

SHAGGY DOG BLUEY

Tied by Peter Coulson

HOOK: Mustad C68S SS, size 2/0
THREAD: White flat waxed
BODY: Sparkleflash belly shine
COLOURING: Crimson red head
EYES: Silver 7 mm 3D self adhesive eyes

The colouring of this fly was based on a very successful pelagic lure. This fly fishes best offshore.

Tied by Peter Coulson

SHAGGY DOG CRAWDAD

HOOK: Mustad C68S SS, size 2/0
THREAD: White flat waxed
BODY: Sparkleflash yellow pearl
COLOURING: Blush pink throat and cheeks, orange warm grey and black back, warm grey and black barbs
EYES: Gold 7 mm 3D self adhesive eyes

This is one of my favourite estuary flathead flies. It is best fished on a floating line in the shallows with a slow, lazy retrieve.

Tied by Peter Coulson

SHAGGY DOG GOLD

HOOK: Mustad C68S SS, size 2/0
THREAD: White flat waxed
BODY: Sparkleflash holographic gold
COLOURING: Black barbs
EYES: Red 7 mm 3D self adhesive eyes

The colouring of this fly was based on a popular lure. This fly fishes best in northern Australia.

Tied by Peter Coulson

SHAGGY DOG PINK THING

HOOK: Mustad C68S SS, size 2/0
THREAD: White flat waxed
BODY: Sparkleflash UV pearl and Shimmerflash micro silver
COLOURING: Sepia barbs and hot pink head
EYES: Silver 7 mm 3D self adhesive eyes

The colouring of this fly was based on the popular Pink Thing. This pattern works extremely well because it presents more naturally. This fly fishes best in northern Australia.

SHAGGY DOG SPOT

HOOK: Mustad C68S SS, size 2/0
THREAD: White flat waxed
BODY: Sparkleflash UV pearl
COLOURING: Bronze and black back, bronze and black spot
EYES: Silver 7 mm 3D self adhesive eyes

Tied by Peter Coulson

SHAGGY DOG WHITEBAIT

HOOK: Mustad C68S SS, size 2/0
THREAD: White flat waxed
BODY: Sparkleflash UV pearl
COLOURING: Cool grey, warm grey, dark green on top
EYES: Silver 7 mm 3D self adhesive eyes

This is my all-time favourite saltwater fly pattern. It is one of those patterns that just works everywhere on any fish, with any retrieve. I have caught more than 50 species on this pattern.

Tied by Peter Coulson

SIMPLE SHRIMP

HOOK: Mustad 34044, Tiemco 811S, Black Magic Salt Water Fly, size 1–2/0
THREAD: Black 3/0 Monocord
TAG: Hot orange dubbing
TAIL: Matched pair of grizzle saddle tips, two strands of Krystal Flash, tied splayed
BODY: Grizzle saddle wound to hook eye, Seducer style

An easy to tie, slow sinking shrimp pattern that can be tied in any colour. Burnt mono eyes can be added for extra effect.

Tied by Chris Beech

Tied by Peter Coulson

SKEETER OFFSHORE

HOOK: Mustad C68S SS, size 2/0
THREAD: White flat waxed
BODY: Sparkleflash belly shine, tied shaggy dog style
COLOUR: 70% grey waterproof marker on the back before you apply SoftDip
EYES: Silver 7 mm self adhesive eyes
OVERBODY: Cover whole fly with two coats of SoftDip

This fly sits in the surface film and leaves a small bow wave with each strip. Only strip this fly in short 10 cm strips with a pause every fifth or sixth strip. Most strikes will occur on the pause. It is best fished around the outer edges of a bait ball that has been smashed up.

Tied by Terry Hayden

SQUID FLY

HOOK: Gamakatsu, size 8/0 or 10/0
THREAD: White flat waxed
TENTACLES: 10–12 white saddle hackles, 2 longer than the others and coated with Softex
BODY: 3/8 inch Flexi cord
BODY EXTENSION: 120lb wire, attach a brass ring to act as a tying point
WINGS: Shaped with 80lb mono, and filled with epoxy
EYES: Large, holographic self adhesive

Tied by Peter Coulson

SQUIDIES BARBED

HOOK: Mustad 34007, size 3/0
THREAD: White flat waxed
BODY: Sparkleflash yellow pearl
COLOURING: Sepia and black barbs
EYES: Gold 7 mm 3D self adhesive eyes
HEAD: 15 mm squid jig

This fly is best fished on a sinking line with a slow retrieve. Using this fly is one of the most enjoyable ways to catch squid.

SQUIDIES RAINBOW

HOOK: Mustad 34007, size 3/0
THREAD: White flat waxed
BODY: Sparkleflash UV pearl
COLOURING: Yellow, orange, purple and indigo blue
EYES: Hot red 7 mm 3D self adhesive eyes
HEAD: 15 mm squid jig

This fly is best fished on a sinking line with a slow retrieve. Using this fly is one of the most enjoyable ways to catch squid.

Tied by Peter Coulson

STARLIGHT

HOOK: Long shank, size 4–8
THREAD: Red mono cord
TAIL: Grey squirrel tail
BODY: Silver gift wrapping cord
UNDERWING: Grey squirrel tail
OVERWING 1: Well-marked wood duck breast feather
OVERWING 2: Natural deer hair
HEAD: Natural deer hair spun and clipped, Muddler style, marked on top with fabric paint pen and underneath with red or pink to give the appearance of gills

This pattern can be fished with both floating and sinking lines. This pattern works best at night time on a floating line with a slow, strip retrieve. Target species are estuary perch, slimy mackerel, flathead, Australian salmon and trout.

Tied by Andrew Lines

TASMAN MINNOW

HOOK: Mustad 34044, 34007, Tiemco 811S, Black Magic Salt Water Fly, size 2–2/0
THREAD: Black flat waxed nylon
BODY: Silver Mylar
COLLAR: Polar Bear PolyBear (or Hivis, Widows Web, Neer Hair)
TOPPING: Two strands each of silver and pearl Krystal Flash then Widows Web (or substitute)
CHEEKS: Three or four strands of silver Sparkleflash, Mylar Motions or Polarflash
EYES: Pearl 2 mm self adhesive eyes, epoxy over

This fly was tied to imitate small baitfish with a thin transparent profile; tie in colour to suit.

Tied by Chris Beech

Tied by Chris Beech

TASMAN WHITEBAIT

HOOK: Kamasan B175, size 6–8
THREAD: White 3/0 Monocord
BODY: Flat pearl Mylar
COLLAR: Polar Bear PolyBear (or HIVIS, Widows Web)
TOPPING: Two strands silver and pearl Krystal Flash, then grey EP Fibres (or HIVIS, Widows Web)
EYES: Silver 1.5 mm self adhesive eyes, epoxy over

This fly was developed for fishing to Tasmania's whitebait feeders.

Tied by Adam Royter

THE GARFISH FLY

HOOK: Wet, size 14
THREAD: Uni 6/0
TAIL: Red marabou
BODY: Deer hair white

This fly was designed to be used in conjunction with a berley trail. It started its life off as just a white deer hair head but quickly grew a red tail through popular demand by the fish.

Tied by Peter Coulson

THE GHOST

HOOK: Mustad 34007, size 1
THREAD: White flat waxed
BODY: Pearl tinsel
LATERAL LINE: Silver Gliss 'N' Glow, two strands each side
OVERWRAP: Slinky Fibre translucent white
OVERWING: Olive Krystal Flash
EYES: Silver 5 mm self adhesive eyes
HEAD: Epoxy

This is a great fly for Australian salmon. Fish on a fast sinking line and strip very fast.

THE McMAGGOT

HOOK: Caddis grub hook, size 12–14
THREAD: Yellow mono cord
UNDERBODY: Lead wire
BODY: White reflective tape, available from automotive and safety equipment suppliers. Lightly coat body with clear nail polish.

This fly is best fished in a flowing tide, where trevally or bream may be prowling for food. It is great with a berley trail.

Tied by Andrew Lines

TWO DOGS

HOOK: Mustad keel hook, size 2/0
THREAD: White flat waxed
BODY: UV pearl Sparkleflash
COLOURING: Bronze and black back, bronze and black spot
EYES: Pearl 4 mm 3D Glow self adhesive eyes

This pattern fishes well around mangroves and structure due to the way that the keel hook works like a weed guard. It also works well fished into large schools of baitfish when large pelagic fish are balling them up.

Tied by Peter Coulson